CAPITAL OF DISCONTENT

CAPITAL OF DISCONTENT

CRIME AND PROTEST IN MANCHESTER'S INDUSTRIAL REVOLUTION

ERIC J. HEWITT

For Sara and Jane

Front cover illustrations, from top: Police Sergeant Charles Brett, shot and killed by Fenians, 1867. (Courtesy of Greater Manchester Police); http://commons.wikimedia.org/wiki/File:Peterloo_Massacre.png. *Back cover illustration:* http://commons.wikimedia.org/wiki/File:Dreadful_Scene_at_Peterloo.png

First published 2014

The History Press
The Mill, Brimscombe Port
Stroud, Gloucestershire, GL5 2QG
www.thehistorypress.co.uk

British Library Cataloguing in Publication Data.
A catalogue record for this book is available from the British Library.

ISBN 978 0 7524 9963 5

Typesetting and origination by The History Press
Printed in Great Britain

CONTENTS

INTRODUCTION

People living in towns like Manchester during the nineteenth century experienced a period of change that was revolutionary in pace and scale. The transfer from medieval to modern, agricultural to industrial, township to urban, transformed their lives in many different ways.

Great opportunities for wealth arose from this Industrial Revolution, which were exploited to their advantage by members of the middle class, who maximised their entrepreneurial spirit and skills in the creation of a new world built on cotton manufacture. Everything else – engineering, canals, railways, factories and urbanisation – followed in its wake.

Those members of the old order who held prestigious positions of power and influence in the local government of the town found their grip on power loosening in the face of a new political class and, despite great efforts to protect their interests, eventually had to yield.

As for those members of the working class employed to work in the factories, herded in the most densely populated, overcrowded and unsanitary conditions, their reaction was predictably confused, violent and demanding of some form of remedial action. However, no matter how squalid their situation, for many it proved to be no worse than what they had left behind in the countryside. Whilst some migrants were attracted to Manchester in the hope that it would provide them with opportunities to work and maintain their families, many were propelled from chronic poverty in the desperate hope that things might get better.

The responses of different groups to this changing environment will be analysed in the following pages, and any identified themes or trends over the period of the nineteenth century will be placed in the context of this Industrial Revolution.

During the first half of the century, the acquisition of wealth and status amongst sections of the middle class was there for all to see. It was proudly on display in the opulent houses built in the suburbs of Didsbury and Withington and in the many grand buildings in the centre of town, which were constructed in the classic style as testimony to success and civic pride – the civic pride having more to do with a pride in wealth creation than anything else.

Within the central districts, not a stone's throw from the magnificent Exchange building, there existed a section of the working-class population that was largely untouched by the benefits of the Industrial Revolution and, within this group, a sub-group whose livelihood was wholly dependent on the proceeds of crime. This criminal class tended to congregate and operate around the public houses that proliferated in the districts of Deansgate, Piccadilly and Market Street. Like the wider society, it was hierarchically structured, with the swell mobsmen at the top and prostitutes and vagrants positioned at the bottom.

Their numbers were boosted by an influx of migrant criminals and vagrants attracted by the many opportunities provided by this new age of commerce and industry. Added to this section of the population were thousands of abandoned children, whose lifestyles were well described by Charles Dickens in his novel *Oliver Twist*. So fearful had these districts become that one visitor to Manchester was moved to describe it as being 'the gateway to hell'.

For the vast majority of the working class, impoverishment and hardship was blamed on heartless employers, and violent protest became their watchword. It took many different forms, with small groups of the unemployed and underemployed taking direct action against employers' property, both at the factory and at private residences, and larger groups, sometimes numbering hundreds and thousands, gathering in public places to demonstrate their frustrations and demand that those in authority heard their pleas and came to their aid. Often, Manchester's working class would send petitions to the Prince Regent in the forlorn hope that he would be sufficiently moved to intervene. Gradually, with guidance from parliamentary reformers like William Cobbett, their protests were refocused and directed towards the reform of parliament. In many respects, parliamentary reform became a kind of panacea for all of their grievances – social, economic and political.

With no effective machinery of local government, an inadequate and ineffective police, and an economy subject to sudden fluctuations – throwing thousands out of work without notice or compensation – the political elite feared that the volatile environment in Manchester and the manufacturing towns was becoming a serious threat to the stability and good order that statesmen and businessmen alike sought to preserve. Convinced that revolution was in the air, the government response was a programme of repression aimed at deterring members of the working class from revolutionary direct action.

As part of the government's response, habeas corpus was suspended; the judicial and penal systems were made even harsher; workers' combinations were prohibited; and military barracks were constructed to encircle the 'most troublesome towns'. In Manchester, the district of Hulme was identified as an appropriate location for stationing both soldiers and cavalry troops, followed a few years later by another huge barracks built at Ashton-under-Lyne, which became known as the Ladysmith Barracks. It must not be overlooked that it was common for the military to police any outbreaks of public disorder, and that the role of the local special constabulary was to provide support. It was not until the 1840s that a reformed, professional police force proved itself capable of taking over the role of the military.

Changes to the environment, work relations, and domestic living standards all impacted on the life chances of Manchester's inhabitants. Population, for example, almost doubled in the first thirty years of the century, whilst housing, sewerage and policing lamentably failed to keep pace. It seems inevitable that frustration gave way to anger among the unemployed and underemployed, who targeted the modern machinery installed in the factories – the main cause of their misery. Politics, for the working class in Manchester, was often the politics of protest in the early nineteenth century.

Influenced by the writings of William Cobbett, this 'Luddite mentality' was gradually rejected by the majority of the working class in favour of parliamentary reform, aimed at widening representation in the growing urban towns at the expense of the 'rotten boroughs'. This shift in ideas and objectives led to growing support of the Chartist movement, trade unionism and, by the end of the century, to the birth of the Labour Party. The Great Reform Act of 1832 turned out to have been a significant building block in this process, as it opened the door, ever so slightly, to greater participation in the political system. The subsequent Reform Acts of 1867 and 1884 extended enfranchisement and secured manhood suffrage for many members of the working class, a process that effectively transformed the political landscape. Of course, it was not until the early twentieth century that women were given a vote.

In many respects, it was multitudinous Manchester, much more than manufacturing Manchester, which gave rise to its reputation as being 'a most dangerous place'. Research carried out by A. Kidd[1] and D.W. Neale[2] concluded that it was the rapid growth in population, overcrowding and urbanisation, rather than the factory system *per se*, that so frustrated its inhabitants that they appeared to be in a constant state of agitation during the first half of the nineteenth century.

Faced with the pressures brought on by rapid population growth on such a scale, Manchester's local government bodies proved unwilling and incapable of addressing the inhabitants' demands and need for change. Their members even resisted and opposed the implementation of the Municipal Corporations Act of 1835 (which empowered local residents to elect borough councils and provided powers for the appointment of a professional police force), going so far as preventing newly elected councillors from accessing local government premises and equipment. This opposition so frustrated the new borough council that its members petitioned the Home Secretary, who agreed to intervene and appoint a Chief Commissioner of Police, with powers to seize control of public premises, levy rates and recruit candidates for a new police force. This embarrassing situation lasted for two years, by which time the opposition had subsided and the old order's protests had effectively evaporated.

The newly elected borough council's first duty under the Act was to appoint a Watch Committee and a new Chief Constable to replace the Chief Commissioner, who by now had returned to London with his new wife and daughter.

Manchester's political leaders were to clash with central government, and particularly with the Home Secretary, on a number of occasions throughout the century, opposing what they perceived to be 'unwarranted government interference in local affairs'. Whether their actions amounted to stubborn intransigence or fierce independence matters not, for this 'little Manchester' attitude was to put at risk the future finances of the town and the ability of its police force to maintain public order.

The huge significance of the town of Manchester in this period cannot be overestimated, and overshadows the developments in other parts of the region, which is the main reason for narrowing the focus at their expense. Of all manufacturing and commercial towns undergoing major changes at this time, Manchester has been chosen because, quite simply, its history is of national, if not international, importance and was seen to be so by many contemporaries. For example, Edward Baines, in his two-volume work entitled *Lancashire*, recorded the social and economic changes that had taken place by 1830. He wrote:

Manchester, as it is one of the ancient towns in Lancashire, so it is one of the most important towns in the kingdom. London, Liverpool and Bristol may claim a superiority as seats of foreign commerce but as a manufacturing station it is unquestionably the metropolis of the British Empire. Out of the £32 million worth of cotton goods produced annually in Great Britain, £20 million worth of this great staple are either actually manufactured here or passed through its markets. In point of population, Manchester ranks second only to London and in opulence probably holds the same rank.[3]

Political ideas and associations were also born out of the social and economic conditions endured in manufacturing Manchester. Harold Perkin claims that between the years 1815 and 1820, a working-class movement was born and that this movement was to go on to develop a working-class consciousness.[4] This process of working-class consciousness was developed through machine-wrecking, trade unionism and collective activity, according to Frederick Engels, who lived and worked in Manchester during the 1840s. He argued that it was not only the birth of a working class that characterised Manchester, but the birth of a conflict between workers and employers that would inevitably result in a revolutionary situation. We now know, of course, that what Engels witnessed taking place in Manchester were not the death throes of capitalism but the beginnings of further economic expansion.[5]

However, to a certain extent this conflict model is undermined by evidence showing that some members of Manchester's bourgeoisie were benevolent and supportive of members of the working class, especially those individuals attempting to lift themselves out of poverty and ignorance. For example, evidence drawn from the research of Foster[6] and Walton[7] identified a 'respectable' section of the working class, supported by the work of Sunday schools, Hampden Clubs, Mechanics' Institutes and Lyceums, and individual benefactors such as Benjamin Heywood.

By 1817, forty Hampden Clubs were established in Manchester with more than 8,000 members.[8] It was an unintended consequence of the prohibitive Combination Acts that so many working men were drawn to these associations. On the face of it, Hampden Clubs operated as working-men's social clubs, where issues of the day were discussed and newspapers read. In reality, however, members often gathered to listen to radical guest speakers covering economic and political issues. A popular guest speaker in Manchester's Hampden Clubs was Samuel Bamford, Middleton's radical poet; and the most popular newspaper read by, or read to, members was Cobbett's *Political Register*.[9]

Members of the governing class, in the early part of the century, focused their attention on events in France and concluded that volatile Manchester had become a seedbed of revolution and, as such, its inhabitants must be repressed at all costs. Alarm bells rang out loud and clear in the corridors of power when it was discovered that in Manchester's Hampden Clubs members of the working class were reading the radical works of Thomas Paine (1791) as well as the writings of William Cobbett. The fact that Cobbett was advocating parliamentary reform through non-violent means provided little comfort or reassurance to a fearful political elite.

To understand the government's response, it has to be appreciated that for politicians of the early nineteenth century, the present constitution was as near perfect as could be, having been settled by the Glorious Revolution of 1688 when William III and Mary replaced James II. The basis of the political constitution included the supremacy of parliament and a system of checks and balances designed to keep control of both the Crown and the common people. Thus, those advocates of parliamentary reform were viewed as radicals and revolutionaries who must be stopped at all costs.

Evidence shows, however, that Manchester's working class were, for the most part, simply demanding that parliament be reformed to their advantage rather than being intent on revolution, as the government had feared. Their stated aims were essentially 'knife and fork' issues, such as improved wages and reduced food prices, rather than the overthrow of the government or the monarchy. In many respects the influences of religion (especially Methodism), social administration and the self-help principles of the co-operative movement have been underestimated when assessing the mindset of Manchester's working class.

In Chapter 1, a description of Manchester in the nineteenth century focuses on the phenomenal expansion of industry and commerce, as well as the severe social and environmental problems left in their wake. This expansion depended on an army of workers and their families, for this was an age when women and children were encouraged to go out to work in the factories for comparatively low wages. Labour was in such demand that people descended on Manchester in huge numbers from the surrounding agricultural counties, and from as far afield as Ireland and even Italy.

In 1801, Manchester's population was estimated to be 84,000, and by 1881 it had risen to 393,000.[10] As the national distribution of population altered in favour of manufacturing towns like Manchester, so too did the source of wealth, as industrial production came to dominate both trade and agriculture. Without doubt, cotton manufacture made Manchester; everything else – commerce, transport, buildings – flowed from the manufacturing process. Not surprisingly, Manchester came to be known as 'cottonopolis'.

It would be misleading, however, to assume that the town of Manchester was born out of the Industrial Revolution. Industrialisation didn't burst forth as a consequence of mechanical inventions such as the introduction of steam power; rather it was the product of a chain of events beginning in Elizabethan times, which gathered pace in the second half of the eighteenth century and accelerated at a pace unprecedented around the beginning of the nineteenth century. Manchester expanded its boundaries throughout the eighteenth century, when the main source of its wealth was derived from the manufacturing of coarse woollens, linens and cotton. Thus, when the factory production of cotton goods began, Manchester was well placed to take advantage and exploit any expansion in demand, due to its skilled workforce, commercial and trading expertise, and the benefits of its location at the confluence of the Irwell, Irk and Medlock rivers. Population and urban growth followed new inventions, which required bigger factories to house the giant steam-powered machinery and both a skilled and non-skilled workforce.

It becomes difficult, therefore, to be precise about a start date for the Industrial Revolution. For practical reasons, this study will begin more or less at the start of the nineteenth century and close around the end of the century. In so many respects, dates are arbitrary, as historical events do not conveniently start and finish on specific dates. Therefore, there will be some overlapping as themes are studied over lengthy periods of time to gain some realistic notion of what was actually taking place. The first half of the century might sometimes seem to be covered disproportionately, but that only reflects the magnitude of changes taking place in that short space of time.

To give some idea of the sheer scale of economic growth that industrialisation had set in motion, Perkin provides some statistics showing that exports of manufactured cotton goods rose tenfold throughout the nineteenth century; imports of raw material, mainly cotton, rose even faster, from around £30 million a year to over £500 million a year; invisibles, such as banking and insurance, grew by almost a hundredfold. Total industrial production grew by as much as fourteenfold.[11]

These figures indicate that the property-owning, entrepreneurial middle class was enjoying untold wealth and prosperity, whereas the vast majority of the population, the working class, continued to endure conditions at work and at home that were unhealthy, cruel and degrading. Factory workers and domestic handloom weavers, in particular, had to face cyclical unemployment and underemployment resulting on the one hand from the vagaries of the market, and on the other from a labour force swelled by migrants and demobbed soldiers arriving home from the wars.

In the first half of the century, outbreaks of violent protest were put down swiftly by the authorities, usually with the aid of the military. There were many examples where protestors sustained serious injuries, which in some cases proved fatal, at the hands of the military. In Chapters 3 and 4, specific examples will be considered and the effectiveness of the government's policies of repression and deterrence will be examined, alongside those critical factors that brought about change and helped restore peace and good order.

Without question, one of the greatest tragedies to hit the people of Manchester occurred on 16 August 1819, when a huge demonstration of workers and their families, drawn from around the region, gathered on St Peter's Field to hear speakers calling for parliamentary reform. The gathering was dispersed by officers and soldiers of the yeomanry and hussars, resulting in 600 people being injured and eleven killed. This tragic event came to be known as the Peterloo Massacre.

Whether any blame could be attached to the Manchester magistrates, the police, the soldiers, or members of the assembled crowd, will be explored in Chapter 3. Valuable evidence provided by eyewitness accounts will be considered, together with the judgement of the court in the case of Redford *v.* Birley (1822), which arose from the actions of Captain Birley and others in the Manchester Yeomanry, who allegedly caused injury to Mr Redford during the demonstration.

A key witness at the trial was Deputy Constable Joseph Nadin, who was in possession of an arrest warrant and had taken the decision not to deploy his special constables into the assembled crowd as previously instructed by the magistrates. It was on his recommendation that the magistrates amended their instructions and called upon troops stationed nearby to assist the police in executing the warrants of arrest issued against the key speakers.

Historically, Joseph Nadin's reputation has been tarnished by allegations that he was a 'brutish and corrupt official', who repeatedly abused his position for monetary gain. 'How else could he afford to retire to the leafy suburbs of Cheadle?' scoffed his arch-critic Archibald Prentice, editor of the *Manchester Gazette*. However, evidence from contemporaries casts doubt on the reliability of such allegations, most of which were politically motivated. Nadin was not a saint, far from it, but in the context of early nineteenth-century Manchester, there is overwhelming evidence to support the view that he was an efficient manager of the two bodies responsible for policing the town, and throughout his twenty years in office he displayed remarkable strength and courage in the face of hostility and considerable danger.

After Peterloo, more and more working people found expression for their grievances through the Chartist movement. Established in 1836, this parliamentary reform movement called upon the government to expand manhood suffrage and create a fairer and more equal voting system for the working class. It peaked in the years leading up to 1848 and then went into a fairly rapid decline. Evidence shows the movement to have been fatally divided between the pacifists and the radicals. Men like Joseph Rayner Stephens were part of the Manchester radical wing, advocating violent rebellion. These public calls to arms led to Stephens' arrest on more than one occasion and gave the movement a 'potential' – but never more than that, for it was never sufficiently co-ordinated or well enough supported to cause the government serious problems. Chartist supporters were far more concerned with economic 'knife and fork' issues than with the overthrow of the political power structure. Its membership peaked when times were hard and then went into decline when economic conditions improved.

One explanation for the non-revolutionary path followed by Manchester's working class was the expansion of religious worship, particularly Methodism. In *Birth of Methodism* (1971), Halévy points out that Methodism was the reason the English working class did not follow the French model of revolution. Other explanations include the influence of middle-class reformers like William Cobbett; the government's 'timely' abolition of the Corn Laws; the popularity of the concept of working-class 'respectability'; and the virtues of hard work, thrift and sobriety, promoted by men like Samuel Smiles in his best-seller *Self-Help* (1859). Engels' prediction that revolution was inevitable failed to materialise, partly due to an underestimation of the willingness of successive governments to adapt and change, and to an upturn in the economy in the second half of the century.

There is little doubt that in the early part of the century, crime in Manchester was considered to have reached a level of violence and frequency far higher than what had gone before, even though meaningful evaluation was frustrated by a lack of statistical evidence. The situation had become intolerable for tradesmen, businessmen and visitors alike, not just in Manchester but in other large towns in the country. Commissions of Inquiry were set up by the government which repeatedly centred their debates on the extent to which criminal behaviour was a consequence of drunkenness, moral turpitude or chronic poverty. However well-meaning, the absence of reliable data frustrated their efforts as they quickly realised that the causes of crime are complex and do not lend themselves to simplistic explanations or solutions. For example, the popularly held view that crime was inextricably linked to economic fluctuations, and that when times were hard the honest section of the labouring poor were reduced to criminality to eke out a living, was seriously undermined by those office-holders whose privileged positions provided a valuable insight. The Rev. J.W. Horsley, prison chaplain, wrote: 'Our prison population in London rises with prosperity and the consequent power of getting drunk. Bad times and the slackness of work in winter produces less crime and not more.'[12]

The identification of trends in crime can be frustrated by the absence of reliable statistics and common understandings of key words and definitions. McCabe warns: 'there is no word in the whole lexicon of legal and criminal law which is so elusive of definition as the word crime.'[13] In attempting to overcome these difficulties, reliance is placed on the assessments and perceptions of informed contemporaries. An example of a reliable source of information is the Rev. Clay, chaplain at Preston prison, where many of Manchesters' convicted criminals were housed. One of the difficulties faced by the authorities was the identification of juvenile offenders who regularly made use of aliases and false birth dates to avoid being classed as adults and repeat offenders.

What is often overlooked is that the history of crime and criminal behaviour is also about the history of power, and how those in positions of power in a society define what action constitutes a crime and what is considered an appropriate punishment. Ideas and attitudes towards crime and punishment changed over the century as the composition of political elites and ideas changed. Harsh reaction and repression gave way to a more compassionate, enlightened penal policy, reflecting a more confident, liberally minded government. In practice, this was a triumph for humanitarian reformers such as Bentham and Howard, and meant punishments, such as hanging and transportation, were replaced by specified terms of imprisonment and the collection of fines.[14]

Any review of the government's repressive agenda must appreciate that in the nineteenth century property was considered sacrosanct by the upper and middle classes. To a great extent, they were influenced by the ideas of John Locke and his *Two Treatises of Government* (1690), which stressed that government has no other end than the preservation of property. As for the property-less labouring poor, however, were they to resort to individual or collective protest they would find themselves at the mercy of a cruel judicial system armed with more than 280 capital offences and the powers of transportation or hard labour for relatively minor crimes against property.

Many contemporaries recognised that great inequalities existed in the criminal justice system. Writers such as Alexis de Tocqueville wrote that 'the criminal justice system was designed to protect the property owning classes and oppress the poor'. Karl Marx and Frederick Engels wrote: 'Private property is exclusive and elitist, its very existence for the few is solely due to its non-existence in the hands of the many.'[15] Engels maintained that criminal behaviour, such as theft, was a form of protest by the working class against a capitalist system that had alienated and exploited them to such an extent that they had become little more than appendages of the factory machine. He viewed the factory, Church and the police as the means by which the state controlled the working class.

A particular concern for the authorities in Manchester was the exceptionally large number of juveniles engaged in all kinds of criminal behaviour. Between the years 1832 and 1835, Manchester police reported that there were 8,650 deserted children roaming the streets of the town and that this number increased at times of economic depression when the cotton factories closed down. The estimated age of an offender was rarely taken into account by the courts, with sentencing equally as harsh and cruel for juveniles as for adults. Records show a 10-year-old girl sentenced to hard labour for wandering the streets at night, and a 10-year-old boy sentenced to ten years' imprisonment and transported for the theft of handkerchiefs.

Among the many migrant groups congregating in the poorer districts, Manchester's Irish community found themselves disproportionately represented in the police and court records of the nineteenth century. Without doubt, drink was the Irishman's weakness and drunkenness was often the precursor of criminal behaviour, according to Manchester's Medical Officer of Health, Dr James Kay. Research suggests that the majority of criminal offences committed by this section of the population were relatively minor in nature, consisting mainly of criminal damage and assaults. However, more recent research reveals that a disproportionate number of convicts hanged for murder at the Strangeways prison were of Irish origin, and that for most of them drink was to blame for their actions.

In the year 1867, Irish politics were transported to the mainland and featured in the Manchester courts when leaders of the Irish Fenian movement were arrested for unrelated offences. En route to Belle Vue prison, the horse-drawn prison van was attacked by Fenian sympathisers and the prisoners were rescued. During the escape, a police sergeant was shot and killed and a constable wounded. In Chapter 8, the main protagonists are identified, as well as members of the local community who courageously came to the aid of the police and assisted in the arrest of several armed Fenian supporters. In many respects this tragic event proved a watershed in Manchester's police–public relations, indicating that attitudes towards the police had changed from the open hostility and suspicion that had marked their introduction in the early 1840s to an acceptance, tolerance and actual support of the idea of a 'people's police'.

One of Manchester's top policemen in the last quarter of the century was Detective Chief Inspector Jerome Caminada, son of an Italian immigrant, who recorded his experiences and observations in a book entitled *Twenty-five Years of Detective Life*. The book is a valuable source of social history, with vivid descriptions of the wretched conditions endured by many of Manchester's labouring poor in a period of so-called prosperity. Revelations that chronic poverty still existed at the end of the nineteenth century attracted national attention when two major reports, published by Booth and Rowntree, highlighted the wretched state of the poor in the cities of London and York and called upon the government to adopt a policy of intervention and support.

In summary, Manchester in the nineteenth century found itself in the eye of the storm that became known as the Industrial Revolution. Environmentally, fields and wastelands were taken over by huge factories, mills and warehouses, rows of terraced housing, navigable canals and railways, which together transformed the township into one of the world's greatest cities. Without doubt, it was cotton manufacture that made modern Manchester, and the wealth and prosperity generated was there for all to see. The political power and influence of the urban middle class followed, as illustrated when Cobden and Bright, the leaders of the Anti-Corn Law League, persuaded Peel to repeal the Corn Laws at the expense of the agricultural interest.

A social consequence of change of such magnitude was the alienation and deprivation of large sections of the working class, whose anger and frustration was manifest in violent acts of criminal damage and public demonstrations demanding reform of the parliamentary system. Beneath this layer of the working class there existed a criminal class, so decadent and ruthless in its own pursuit of wealth that men of commerce and trade became fearful of visiting this 'most dangerous place'.

By the second half of the century, contemporaries viewed the city as a 'very much quieter place', thanks to sustained economic growth, except for a period in the 1860s when the cotton famine threw thousands out of work. But this was to prove the pinnacle of Manchester's success, as competitors, at home and abroad, began to catch up and overtake this 'capital of industry'.

It is no accident that critics of the Industrial Revolution were in the ascendancy in the first half of the century, and its supporters in the second. The issues and problems, of course, arose in the beginning and the solutions and actions to tackle them came as a response. What follows is offered as a contribution to the knowledge and understanding of a period in our history that is not long past. Like all social histories it is selective, with some events and characters omitted on the grounds that they are not felt to be representative or particularly relevant. Any errors to be found are mine alone.

Notes

1. A. Kidd, *Manchester*, 1993.
2. W.B. Neale, *Juvenile Delinquency in Manchester*, 1840, p.58.
3. E. Baines, *Lancashire*, Vol.2, 1824, p.57.
4. H. Perkin, *The Origins of Modern English Society*, 1969, p.3.
5. F. Engels, *The Condition of the Working Class in England*, 1892.
6. J. Foster, *Class Struggle and the Industrial Revolution*, 1974.
7. J.K. Walton, *Lancashire*, 1987, p.154.
8. J. Rule, *The Labouring Classes*, p.274.
9. J.K. Walton, *Lancashire*, 1987, p.154.
10. E. Baines, *Lancashire*, 1824, p.128.
11. H. Perkin, *The Origins of Modern English Society*, 1969, p.3.
12. J.W. Horsley, *Jottings from Jail*, 1887, p.57.
13. S. McCabe, 'Crime', article in D. Walsh and A. Poole (eds), *A Dictionary of Criminology*, 1983.
14. V.A.C. Gatrell, 'Crime, Authority and a Police State', 1983.
15. K. Marx and F. Engels, *The Communist Manifesto*, 1844.

I

MANCHESTER IN THE NINETEENTH CENTURY: SITE AND SETTING

For practical reasons, we begin by placing Manchester in the context of social and economic changes taking place in the nineteenth century, the nature and degree of which have been described as 'revolutionary'. Examples of the changes experienced by those living and working within Manchester's boundaries include: rapid growth in the population; relative freedoms enjoyed by migrants previously shackled by feudalism; inventions of the age which transformed methods of working and travelling; and the emergence of two great classes, a middle class of wealth and prosperity and an industrial working class doomed to hardship and suffering.

These changes shaped the ideas of the period. In the early years, protection and regulation favoured the agricultural and landed interests at the expense of the industrial middle and working classes. An obvious example is the passing of the Corn Laws, which protected the profits of those associated with agriculture at the expense of everyone else.

Manchester's inhabitants were totally dependent on the manufacture and sale of cotton goods. The manufacturing process was completely revolutionised as a result of brilliant inventions by Arkwright, Hargreaves and Crompton, along with the application of Watt's rotative steam engine. Large-scale factory building to house the giant machinery changed the landscape by concentrating manufacturing and warehousing within town boundaries and away from traditional locations alongside riverbanks.

Hargreaves' spinning jenny, invented in 1764, was the very first of the inventions to effectively change the social and economic position of the working class. The original machines were housed in domestic cottages, but as the number of spindles increased they were rehoused in purpose-built factories. Arkwright's water-frame (so called because it was driven by water power) and Crompton's mule hastened the trend towards factory production and urbanisation at the cost of the domestic workforce.

Towards the end of the eighteenth century, Manchester had already drawn large factories to its riverbanks, including Garrett and Pendleton's mill on the Irk, Banks' mill on the Irwell, and David Holt's mill on the Medlock at Ancoats. The first purpose-built mills located in the heart of Manchester were built in the early 1780s for Richard Arkwright – the inventor: one in Miller Street, Ancoats, and another in Shudehill. The first to be powered by Watt's steam engine was erected in Auburn Street, Piccadilly, for Peter Drinkwater. In the early nineteenth century, Drinkwater employed a young Robert Owen as his mill manager. Owen went on to start his own factory in Chorlton-on-Medlock before moving to the New Lanark mills, owned by his father-in-law, where he developed his now-famous co-operative ideas. It is widely acknowledged that Owen's ideas on cooperation and socialism inspired Marx and Engels, the Chartists and the co-operative movement.

The biggest of Manchester's cotton factories by the early nineteenth century was reputedly that owned by McConnel and Kennedy in Ancoats, which was six storeys tall. George and Adam Murrays' mill, also in Ancoats, housed 1,215 operatives, and another three mills in Manchester employed between 800 and 1,000.[1] In neighbouring Salford stood Watt and Boulton's imposing mill, which was seven storeys tall, each floor being lit by gas burners and mantles. One visitor in 1814 commented: 'It is impossible to describe the magnificent appearance of a mill with 256 windows all alight as though brilliant sunshine was streaming through them.'[2]

Giant factories such as these, however, were the exception rather than the rule. Gatrell points out: 'Giant factories did not dominate the cotton manufacturing industry. During the first half of the century, only 3 per cent of cotton factories employed more than 1,000. Forty-three per cent employed fewer than 100.'[3]

The Murray's mill stood next to the old Ancoats Hall in Every Street, a black-and-white timbered building that was the ancestral home of the Lord of the Manor, Sir Oswald Mosley. The Mosley family were London-based merchants who purchased the manor of Manchester in 1596 as an ideal location for conducting business in the wool trade.[4]

It is evident that Manchester's inhabitants were already skilled in wool and cotton manufacture long before the beginning of the nineteenth century.

A survey of the North West conducted in 1773 found that the small township of Manchester contained many small factories, and domestic workers making woollen hats and weaving coarse woollen fabrics. The report revealed that there were 311 houses, 361 families, 947 males and 958 females resident within its boundaries.[5]

By 1816, Manchester housed eighty-six steam-powered factories, most of them located around Ancoats, Oxford Street, New Cross and Beswick. A similar number of warehouses were concentrated in the town centre, with no less than fifty-seven warehouses listed around the area of Cannon Street. Spin-off industries, such as building and engineering, were also booming, with specialist engineers such as Nasmyth, inventor of the steam hammer, and Whitworth, with his standard screw threads, at the forefront.

An example of the entrepreneurial spirit in engineering is provided by William Fairbairn, who started out in the High Street, in partnership with James Willie, in 1817. The two men then set up an ironworks in Canal Street, Ancoats, which employed 300 men. Not only did they supply ironwork to local factories, they also developed a thriving export business supplying iron to Russia, Turkey and Sweden.

Transport was another important spin-off, with canal construction absorbing large numbers of able-bodied men. It started in the second half of the eighteenth century with the Manchester–Rochdale Canal, followed by links to Bolton/Bury; Ashton-under-Lyne/Huddersfield; and then on to Stockport and the Peak District. The principal cargoes were cotton, woollens, coal, stone and timber. The Rochdale Canal Company's prosperity grew rapidly alongside industry and commerce. In 1829, tonnage was 500,000, and ten years later it had risen to 875,000. Toll receipts rose correspondingly from £38,000 to £62,000 in the year 1839.[6]

It is extremely difficult to be precise when dating the beginning of the period we now know as the Industrial Revolution, simply because economic growth is at first a slow, cumulative process that takes time to reach the critical point at which further advance requires a change of structure. As Adam Smith explained in 1776, 'Since the time of Henry VIII, the wealth and revenue of the country have been continually advancing and, in the course of their progress, their pace seems rather to have been gradually accelerated than retarded. They seem not only to have been going on, but to have been going faster and faster.'

Signs of a significant growth in the economy were present in the late seventeenth century, sufficient to suggest an Industrial Revolution was imminent. According to Perkin, an upturn in all the curves of growth around

1745 'produced no immediate change in the fundamental structure of the economy and society but may be regarded as the initial acceleration of the run-up for take-off'.[7]

By the beginning of the nineteenth century, Manchester was in the process of being transformed and extended on all sides to accommodate demands for labour, factories and transportation. King Street, for example, had been cut through to Deansgate; Piccadilly was a broad space of land that contained the infirmary and a large pond surrounded by iron railings; Mosley Street, named after the Lord of the Manor, was the most fashionable residential street in the whole town; and Tib Street was divided and named Stable Street at its Piccadilly end, probably because it ran alongside the back of the Bridgewater Arms, the town's principal coaching house. Corporation Street did not exist in the early nineteenth century, and most of Oxford Street and beyond was gardens and fields.

The upper end of Market Street and St Ann's Square contained private dwellings. Between Oldham Road and Rochdale Road, the ground was open and the imposing St George's Church stood by itself. Bradford Road was marked out for construction but not yet built and Mill Street, then called Hallsworth Street, had only a few houses. Great Ancoats Street was built only as far as Port Street, and the old Ancoats Hall stood alone at the end of Every Street.[8]

To facilitate transport in and out of the town, the Police Commissioners announced in 1826 their intention to build a new bridge across the Irwell at Ducie Street on the Salford boundary. Seven years later, after the collapse of the supporting wall opposite the cathedral at Hunts Bank, they set about a major road-widening scheme which included a new river wall alongside the Irwell. It was opened in 1839, two years after Queen Victoria came to the throne; therefore, it seemed appropriate to name it the Victoria Bridge.[9]

The social consequences of this fairly rapid economic growth were largely unchecked and unregulated. For the vast majority of inhabitants, living conditions were squalid, damp, cramped and unhealthy. Their many deprivations were vividly described by Dr James Phillips Kay, Medical Officer of Health, after he had visited the Little Ireland district, now known as Granby Row, in 1832:

> The upper rooms are with few exceptions very dirty and the cellars much worse, all damp and some occasionally overflowed. The cellars consist of two rooms on a floor each nine to ten feet square. Some were inhabited by ten persons others by even more. In many, the people had no beds and

keep each other warm by stowage of shavings, straw etc., a change of linen or clothes is an exception to the common practice. Many of the backrooms where they sleep have no other means of ventilation than the front door of the front rooms. To these fertile sources of disease were sometimes added the keeping of pigs and other animals.

Manchester, properly so-called, is chiefly inhabited by shopkeepers and the labouring classes. Those districts in which the poor dwell are of recent origin. The rapid growth in cotton manufacture has attracted operatives from every part of the kingdom, and Ireland has poured forth the most destitute of her hordes to supply the constantly increasing demand for labour. Near the centre of the town a mass of buildings inhabited by prostitutes and thieves, is intersected by narrow and loathsome streets and courts defiled by refuse. These nuisances exist in No.13 district on the western side of Deansgate, and chiefly abound in Wood Street, Spinning Field, Cumberland Street, Parliament Passage, Parliament Street and Thomson Street. In Parliament Street, there is only one privy for 380 inhabitants, which is placed in a narrow passage where its effluvia infest the adjacent houses and must prove a most fertile source of disease.[10]

Angus Bethune Reach revisited these districts a decade later and found little had changed in the intervening years. Describing the Ancoats district, he wrote: 'Along the great thoroughfare called Oldham Road and in the centre of Ancoats itself are situated the most squalid of streets, inhabited by swarms of the most squalid looking people which I have ever seen.' Commenting on the supply of water in the poorer districts, Reach drew upon the Chief Constable's report of 1847. He wrote:

By the returns, it appears that the number of streets, alleys, squares etc. within the borough was 2,955. The number of dwelling houses 46,922. Of these that were supplied with piped water numbered 11,190; while not less than 12,776 houses derived their water from a common cock or tap in the street. The number of houses which reaped no advantage, either from pipes or from taps in the street was nearly as great as the amount of dwellings provided for in both of these ways, being 22,956. The number of cellar dwellings was 5,070 and of these only 1,408 were provided with piped water.

With a direct swipe at some of Manchester's middle class, Reach observed: 'The mill owners of Manchester have paid, until recently, little or no attention to the state of the dwellings of their workpeople.'[11]

From 1835, the Manchester Statistical Society began to publish information that was critical of the social conditions in the town. Highlighting the state of social housing, one report read:

> Cheap jerry-built housing, usually consisting of two rooms, one above the other, and with walls often only one brick thick, might be inhabited by a family of seven or more. In the three storey houses at 46 and 48 Back Irk Street, for example, lived twenty two people. Cellars of houses were often let out to other families or to lodgers; at 4 St John Street (another cellar dwelling) there were eight members of the Reilly family and eleven lodgers.[12]

In the Statistical Society's report dated 1842 and entitled 'The Sanitary Conditions of the Labouring Population of Great Britain', Manchester's figures were compared with Rutland, so as to highlight the differences in mortality rates:

Classification	Average Age at Death	
	Manchester	Rutland
Professional	38	52
Tradesmen	20	41
Mechanics, Labourers	17	38

It should be noted that the exceptionally high number of infant deaths in Manchester contributed to these abnormal figures.

The inequalities of life were not only to be found in the industries and factories but in the workers' access to public services. The report noted: 'The expense of cleaning the streets in Manchester is £5,000 per annum. For this sum, the first class of streets, namely those occupied by the most opulent, are cleansed once a week, the second class once a fortnight and the third class once a month.'

Factory operatives also faced untold misery and hardship at their place of work; the situation was so bad that it was reported that some children were driven to commit suicide.[13] In March 1827, the Manchester firm of Thackery & Russell was fined £20 for employing a 6-year-old girl as a scavenger in the spinning-room for 1s 6d a week. The girl worked from 5.45 a.m. to 10.15 p.m. She and the other children employed were allowed half an hour for breakfast and an hour for dinner, 'but they took their tea by snatches as the work went on', reported one witness, who said that he frequently saw children at the mill nod-off over their machines 'as if unable to keep on their feet'.

In another example, a correspondent to the *Lancashire & Yorkshire Co-operator*, published in April 1832, described an occasion when he and a friend were returning home from a public dinner at two o'clock in the morning and observed a girl of 7 years of age shivering with cold at the gates of a factory waiting for her shift to start. According to the Factory Act of 1833, no less than 87 per cent of children aged between 10 and 15 were employed in factories in the manufacturing towns of Lancashire. Under the revised terms of this new legislation, children had to be 9 years old before they could be employed and, as they were supposed to attend a factory school for two hours a day, their actual working hours were limited to eight. However, a lack of factory schools and teachers meant that in practice this provision was rarely met.

Notwithstanding these shocking descriptions of factory life in towns like Manchester, migrants still poured in from the rural areas, often leaving behind conditions that were even worse. During his tour of the manufacturing districts of Lancashire in 1842, Cooke-Taylor wrote:

> The most striking phenomenon of the factory system is the amount of population which it has suddenly accumulated on certain points. There has long been a continuous influx of operatives from other parts of Britain, these men have very speedily laid aside all their old habits and associations to assume those of the mass in which they are mingled. The manufacturing population is not new in its formation alone, it is new in its habits of thought and action, which have been formed by the circumstances of its condition with little instruction and less guidance from external sources. However severe the conditions may be, there is a something behind which he dreads more. The factory system is therefore preferred to the more usual conditions of labour by the population which it employs.[14]

For the pace and scale of the Industrial Revolution to be sustained, it required – in addition to all the economic factors – a delicate adjustment of population growth. That just such an adjustment took place at the end of the eighteenth century and early nineteenth century is now largely acknowledged without much dispute. Manchester's population started to grow at an alarming rate in the second half of the eighteenth century. In 1774, it was estimated at 41,000, rising to 84,000 by 1801, at the time of the first census. In 1821, it was 123,000; in 1831, it was 187,000; in 1841, 237,646; in 1851, 316,243; in 1861, 357,979; in 1871, 379,374; and in 1881, 393,358, according to the parliamentary census returns. Similar increases were reported between the years 1801 and 1831 in the satellite townships of Oldham: 21,000 to 38,000; Bolton: 29,000 to 50,000; and Blackburn: 32,000 to 53,000.

This pattern of growth was remarkably similar to that of Liverpool, even though founded on very different economic bases. In Manchester, factories and warehouses encapsulated the newer way of life, whereas in Liverpool the dominance of the docks meant that work was essentially casual and unskilled. Both towns relied to a great extent on cotton manufacture, and the import and export of raw materials and finished goods.

These changes, however, were not general across the country but represented a redistribution in favour of areas like Manchester. At the beginning of the eighteenth century, the most populous counties were Middlesex, Somerset, Gloucester and Wiltshire. By the nineteenth century, they were being replaced by Lancashire, West Riding of Yorkshire, Staffordshire and Middlesex. And within these counties, the cotton towns were growing the fastest, followed by coal- and iron-producing towns, which in many cases were the same.[15]

Historians have locked horns for some time over the causes of this rise in population. In the early nineteenth century, the traditional view was that any rise in population equated to a rise in prosperity. This view was challenged by Thomas Malthus, who argued that unless a rising population can be sustained by advances in agricultural production, then sooner or later it spelt disaster and suffering for the poor as food supplies dwindled. Before the onset of the Industrial Revolution came the agricultural revolution, which involved land enclosures and intensive crop growth, followed by improvements in food production, which were to prove crucial in enabling the demand from the expanding manufacturing towns to be sustained.[16]

Alternative explanations for a rise in population can be divided into two schools of thought. On the one hand, it is claimed that the rise was due mainly to a fall in the death rates brought about by medical improvements, such as hospitals and trained medical staff. Others argue that the rise in population was due to a rise in the birth rate, and that this was brought about by earlier marriages and an increase in the number of marriages – both of which were linked to economic improvements, plus an increase in the number of churches being built.

Another factor not in dispute is the number of people coming into Manchester as migrants. Workers in declining trades, such as handloom weaving and agricultural labouring, often travelled relatively short distances, attracted by the prospect of improved wages and regular employment. In 1824, when agricultural wages in the North West averaged 11s per week, factory workers in Manchester were receiving on average 13s per week.[17]

Skilled female labour made up a significant part of the migrant streams, with women textile workers often abandoning work at home for factory work, where their skills were in great demand. Female factory workers provided factory owners with a cheap labour force, with many women operatives being paid only half that of their male colleagues.

In the beginning of the nineteenth century, migrants into Manchester included many Italians, who formed a vibrant community in the New Cross and Ancoats areas, which became known as Little Italy. They were mostly craftsmen such as carvers, gilders, cabinet makers and precision engineers, making barometers and thermometers for the newly rich merchants and manufacturers. Later, a second wave of Italians arrived with famous names like the Granellis, Sivoris, Gerards and Schiavos, some of them famous for making and selling ice cream.

After 1815, with the collapse of the Irish economy, waves of Irish workers arrived and settled around the Ancoats area. They were joined in the period 1845–51 by another wave of distressed workers in the wake of the Great Famine. Opportunities for unskilled labour were in abundance, particularly in road, canal and rail construction. By this time, the number of Irish born in Manchester was estimated at 17 per cent of the population, compared to around 10 per cent in the rest of Lancashire. In the poorer districts like Ancoats, Collyhurst and New Cross, they numbered 34 per cent of the population.[18]

Often, the Irish migrants found themselves marginalised and ostracised by many native workers, who not only feared for their jobs but associated these Irish migrants with the worst excesses of drunkenness and violence that so characterised the inner districts of the town and had given it such a bad reputation.

In terms of labour effect, the impact of Irish settlement is difficult to assess with any accuracy, with historians disagreeing as to the wider economic and social implications. E.H. Hunt,[19] for example, argues that the number of Irish migrants moving into the Lancashire towns actually kept wage rates low at the expense of local workers. On the other hand, J.G. Williamson[20] contends that the numbers were not great enough to influence wage rates. However, this argument appears flawed in so far as it represents an over-reliance on national statistics, which tend to distort the true picture in towns like Manchester, where high numbers of Irish migrants placed considerable strains not only on wages but on housing and policing.

What is clear is that Irish workers played a critical role in the success of the Industrial Revolution in the North West. However, members of Manchester's working class did not always see it that way, particularly when times were hard; in such times, the Irish were singled out as scapegoats. This was illustrated in Elizabeth Gaskell's novel *Mary Barton* (1848), when striking mill workers in Manchester were moved to violence by the threat from 'footsore, way-worn, half-starved imports from Ireland and the outlying districts'. And in *North and South* (1854), Gaskell describes a factory in which local workers riot because of the introduction of Irish workers.

The 'labour effect' was further complicated by the return of thousands of demobbed soldiers from the French wars, who were in search of employment, and by the impact of blockades and counter-measures. In a speech in parliament in 1809, Whitbread pointed out that, as a consequence of the blockades, 'our imports of cotton had fallen by 27 million and 32 cotton mills in Manchester were stood idle'.[21]

The migrant workers placed a tremendous burden on the local bodies charged with the tasks of public health and policing. That they were struggling to cope was much in evidence; James Whitaker observed at the end of the eighteenth century that Manchester was 'beginning to be regarded as the centre of widespread and deeply ramified social disorganisation'.[22] Phyllis Deane later reported:

> The towns had been outgrowing the existing technology for urban living and it is fair to say that in most urban areas the human environment was deteriorating perceptively through the first half of the century. By the 1820s the old moulds of economic and social behaviour were being rapidly broken before the new moulds had begun to set. The country as a whole was ill-prepared for the problems emerging, and as a consequence there was a building-up of tension.[23]

Gradually, the government introduced reforms by way of the Municipal Corporations Act of 1835, which effectively did away with the old medieval systems of public administration. All too often, however, the government's responses in this period were driven by a fear of revolt rather than benevolence or genuine concern. The Hammonds wrote:

> The shock of the French Revolution brought with it a new way of looking at the mass of the nation. The people, especially in the new and growing towns, looked to be a threat, a potentially dangerous force capable of overthrowing

the existing order. As a consequence, the attitude of the government hardened, public meetings were suppressed, political reformers persecuted.[24]

The government saw useful allies in the middle class for keeping the working class under control. Ignoring calls for a reform of parliament and improvements to working and living conditions, they set down repressive legislation with the support of commercial and manufacturing interests. The Combination Acts, for example, set out to prohibit workers from combining to effect changes in their conditions at work. Workmen were to obey their masters as they would the state, and the state was to enforce the master's demands as it would its own. All actions made in defence of their common interests were prohibited. The Combination Acts were in force for a quarter of a century, and during that time the workpeople were at the mercy of their masters. Many were hauled before the courts for protesting at the harsh treatment being meted out.

An example that occurred at Stockport in 1816 was reported to the committee set up to examine the functioning of artisans and machinery. Joseph Sherwin gave evidence that he was a factory worker in Stockport where the average wage was 8s a week for a fourteen-hour day. The factory owner announced that he was reducing wages to 3d per loom for providing 'artificial light'. This reduction amounted to 6d a week for most workers, but in some cases it amounted to 9d. In the summer months, when lighting was not a problem, the master 'forgot to restore the deducted amounts in the workers' wages'. The situation was made worse when winter returned, as the master announced that he was making further deductions for artificial lighting. The workers objected and decided they would walk out on strike. Twelve men and eleven women were singled out and taken before the Magistrates' Court, charged under the Combination Acts, and each one received a sentence of one month's imprisonment.[25]

The growth of masters and a managerial class at the beginning of the nineteenth century attracted men with little previous experience of manufacturing, who had saved or borrowed enough to start out in business. Often they would engage in joint enterprises with two or three partners. Richard Arkwright, for example, helped build the early spinning and carding machines and then went on to build and manage huge factories without any previous experience. Yeomen such as Robert Peel (father of the prime minister) invested money made from farming and coal mining into manufacturing in Bury.[26]

The Manchester manufacturer of the nineteenth century was summed up by Charles Dickens in his novel *Hard Times* (1854). 'Thomas Gradgrind was eminently practical. A man of realities. A man of facts and calculations and nothing more. Ready to measure any parcel of human nature, and tell you what it comes to.' The *Pictorial Times* newspaper (1843) similarly reported:

> Generally speaking, your manufacturer is a plodding man of business who is to be found in his counting house at hours when his Liverpool or London rival is snugly reposing in the bosom of his family. The complaint against the majority of Manchester men is well founded, that they are so engrossed in business [as] to have little time and inclination for the more elegant pursuits of life.[27]

However, the available evidence suggests that such descriptions of Manchester's manufacturers and businessmen were inaccurate. For example, as early as 1781 the Manchester Literary & Philosophical Society was founded for the advancement of knowledge and the exchange of ideas. It attracted members from the Heywood and Phillips banking families, and major manufacturing families such as the Gregs and the McConnels. In 1823, the Royal Manchester Institution was founded, which later became the Manchester Arts Gallery, attracting many famous arts exhibitions and collections. In 1835, the Athenaeum Club was founded and put on talks from outstanding speakers, including Disraeli, which attracted manufacturers and businessmen from across the region. The Portico Library was built in Mosley Street in 1806 and attracted almost 1,000 members. The Rylands Library and Owens College (the forerunner of the University of Manchester) can be added to the list of societies, clubs and institutions that enriched the town's cultural heritage and challenged the popular myth that Manchester's new middle class was ignorant in culture, art and 'the more elegant pursuits of life'.

To understand the harsh and reactionary zeal pursued by many masters and members of the governing class, it has to be acknowledged that in the early nineteenth century it appeared the most natural thing in the world that the economic structure should resemble the political structure, and that in the mill, as in the state, power should be concentrated in the hands of a few men who were to act and think for the rest. This attitude was well described by Adam Smith in his *Wealth of Nations* (Book 5). He wrote: 'Civil government, so far as it is instituted for the security of property, is, in reality, instituted for the defence of the rich against the poor, or of those who have some property against those who have none at all.'

By 1818, the government was Tory, as it had been for the previous two decades, with just one brief interlude of coalition. The prime minister was the 2nd Earl of Liverpool, Robert Banks Jenkinson. Reaction was a shadow that hung over the whole period. A false parallel was drawn with the French Revolution and, having drawn it, the Tory government stuck with it. To give an inch to the labouring poor would result in the same pattern being followed in England as in France, it was argued.

And yet, this assessment of Manchester's working class was fundamentally flawed. Evidence suggests that, with few exceptions, workers were essentially loyal to 'Church and King'. Their intention was not to destroy or dismantle the existing political structure but to secure changes through parliament that would benefit them economically. As early as 18 January 1819, a political meeting held in Manchester passed a declaration calling for three basic reforms: annual parliaments, universal suffrage and the repeal of the Corn Laws. In the following months, a number of Political Union meetings were held across Manchester that united the working class behind this reform programme. Calls for a reform of parliament, as articulated by William Cobbett and Henry Hunt, were later enshrined in the charter of reform supported by the Chartist movement.

Radical ideas and protestations, however, were not the exclusive preserve of the urban working class. Agricultural labourers in the southern counties were described in the 1830s as being 'infested by radical ideas of the worst kind', and villages were described as 'hotbeds of sedition'. Protests indicated that a change had taken place in the traditional farmer–labourer relationship, which had shifted from one of paternalism to one that was finance-driven in response to the demands from manufacturing towns for greater quantities of foodstuffs at affordable prices. These changes in the countryside partly explain the great exodus of labouring families, propelled by the distressed rural conditions to search for a 'better life' in manufacturing towns like Manchester.

To sum up so far, the first half of the nineteenth century saw a running debate about the constitution of a political system undergoing a rapid and fundamental change. The parliamentary reform movement was seeking to change the present system to include and benefit the middle and working classes. Ideas put forward by William Cobbett were considered to be more 'British' and pragmatic than the revolutionary ideas put forward by Thomas Paine, which were associated with the 'French' uprising. It must be remembered, however, that the country had just been extricated from a bloody war with France, during which the French had planned to invade Britain, until they were thwarted by the Duke of Wellington and his army.

By mid-century, Manchester was on the threshold of becoming a truly great industrial city, with industries such as engineering, building, iron-founding, bleaching and dyeing all rising alongside cotton manufacture. There was a vigorous domestic trade and an even more profitable export trade, linked to the port of Liverpool. Manufactured cotton goods accounted for almost half of the country's visible exports in the first half of the century. Commerce and trade were fast becoming as important to Manchester's prosperity as cotton manufacturing. The expansion of banking, insurance, warehousing and the rebuilt Exchange in Deansgate demonstrated the value and wealth of commercial enterprise in the town. According to the census returns of 1841, only around 20 per cent of the workforce was employed in cotton factories, with many more employed in the building industry, commerce, transport and domestic service.

However, this prosperity had fragile foundations, with 'business panics' becoming part of the now familiar cycle of 'boom and bust' carried over from earlier decades. There were periodic shortages of raw cotton (the most pressing being during the years of the cotton famine of 1861–65) and there was increasing competition from cotton-manufacturing countries across Europe and North America. Notwithstanding, Manchester continued to dominate the world's cotton trade throughout the decades and up to the outbreak of the First World War in 1914, but its dominance was only temporary.

People from most sections of Manchester society profited from long periods of economic prosperity. Between the years 1875 and 1895, for example, a sharp fall in prices of both industrial goods and agricultural produce raised the living standards of many working-class families; the world's markets once again opened up to trade, with textiles, engineering, railways and commerce very much at the forefront of profit-making enterprises. Wages also rose from an index number of 100 in 1850 to 159 in 1874, and to 166 in 1895. At the same time, working hours were reduced from an average of sixty hours to fifty-four hours per week, with the majority of workers now enjoying Saturday afternoons off work. This resulted in greater opportunities for leisure and sports, both as participants and spectators, all of which meant that the working class in Manchester was being described by observers as 'a kindlier and healthier people', less prone to violent behaviour, drunkenness and disorder.[28]

Politically, what many observers believed to have been a significant breakthrough took place at the Free Trade Hall on 3 April 1872, when Benjamin Disraeli, leader of the Conservative Party, announced, 'The people of England would be idiots if they should not have long perceived that the time has come when social not political improvement is the object which they ought to pursue.' Disraeli went on to lead a victorious Conservative Party in the general election of 1874, and introduced a range of social measures, including the Pure Food and Drugs Act, the Artisans' Dwellings Act, and the Factory Act, in the first twelve months of government. While Disraeli claimed he had 'settled the long and vexatious contest between capital and labour and gained for the Tories the lasting affection of the working class', his social reform programme was not especially far-reaching and anything but substantial. Members of the working class had to wait until 1906 before a Liberal government introduced major state-funded benefits in what became known as the 'people's budget'.[29]

Despite the visible signs of wealth and prosperity in the streets and buildings in the city centre of Manchester, the city's labouring poor continued to congregate around the central districts of Deansgate, Angel Meadow, Collyhurst and Ancoats, impervious to the so-called benefits of industrialisation that others enjoyed. Social surveys carried out in the period of the cotton famine found that at least 25 per cent of the inhabitants of Manchester and Salford were in primary poverty, and, though definitions might vary, the labouring poor continued to be in dire need of help and support. For many, survival meant clothing and items of furniture being sold at pawnshops, savings withdrawn, and rooms for rent given up as many families went to the parish for relief.[30]

Writing about the social conditions that existed in the 1870s, Detective Chief Inspector Caminada revealed deprivations similar to those described by Dr Kay in the 1830s:

> Travelling along Charter Street and Angel Meadow, the exterior of these houses presents a dingy face of crumbling brick, begrimed by the soot of years. The elevation consists of three storeys, the first two are lighted by windows which denote unmistakeable antiquity and multifarious are the methods employed to refuse wind and rain admittance. On entering, the apartment is full of men and women, though the former predominate. Some are seated on broken-backed chairs or upon dilapidated stools ranged around a filthy table, most of the occupants are devouring various kinds of messes washed down by tea, coffee or beer. The room reeks, the whole scene is squalid and cheerless. Yet no sense of shame is visible on the countenances of the motley inhabitants.[31]

By the 1870s, Manchester's population had reached 379,374 (compared to 237,646 in 1843), with large numbers crowded in areas so small that the official density figure was put at 83.6 per acre, compared with Salford's figure of just 23.5, Birmingham's 47.2 and London's 41.2.

Writing in the *Sunday Chronicle* on 5 May 1889, Robert Blatchford pointed out: 'In Manchester, we found that there were slums of courts, back to backs and alleys everywhere that had not changed in the previous 50 years.' An illus-

trative example of what life was like for the labouring poor of Manchester at
the end of the century is provided by Tom Haddock, who was born in 1899,
near to the London Road station, which now forms part of today's Piccadilly
station. At 18 months old, his family moved to No. 2 Court, Stand Street, off
Store Street, Ancoats, in the midst of the stables and warehouses below the
station platforms:

> In our family, including my mother and father, there were ten of us. There
> was not one of us children born in the same house. Every eighteen months
> we moved, sometimes to get rid of the landlord when we couldn't pay the
> rent. All were born in Ancoats though. My dwelling had neither taps, gas or
> electricity and the toilet was located at the end of the row of houses.[32]

By contrast, Manchester's middle class contained a wealthy, powerful elite, 'an
urban aristocracy' made up of bankers, merchants and industrialists, many of
them drawn from a narrow section of Methodists, Unitarians and Quakers
who worshipped at the Cross Street and Mosley Street chapels. Ten out of the
city's first twenty mayors were drawn from the Cross Street chapel alone. In
the general election of 1857, for example, John Bright, the Free Trade reformer,
suffered defeat at the hands of John Potter of the Potter dynasty, whose Potter
and Norris warehouses were the largest for miles around. The second victorious candidate was James Aspinall Turner, a cotton manufacturer. Both Potter
and Turner worshipped at the Cross Street chapel and enjoyed the support of
the *Manchester Guardian*, whose editor, John Taylor, was also a member of the
congregation, as well as being a member of the Friends Meeting House.[33]

This new order filled the political void created by the desertion of the
old gentry families (such as the Mosleys and the de Traffords) to pastures
green. There were many successful manufacturing families who also deserted
the smoke-filled stench of the city for the fresh air of the countryside and
the seaside. Recalling her family's removal to a new life in Alderley Edge,
Katherine Chorley, daughter of the managing director of the engineering
firm of Mather & Platt, wrote: 'Our life has now become sharply differenti-
ated and quite opulent.'

By the end of the century, Manchester's new order of businessmen and
industrialists was determined not to stand still but to forge ahead into new
markets around the world. Faced with increasing competition from overseas,
a committee set up to review the situation concluded that the add-on costs
of transport, warehousing and port charges in Liverpool all contributed to
making them increasingly uncompetitive. Inspired by the construction of the

Suez Canal in 1869, it was decided to form another committee, led by John Adamson, to examine the feasibility of opening up inland Manchester to the seas and oceans of the world. Their vision and determination led to the construction of the Manchester Ship Canal, which linked the city with Liverpool and the open seas. The canal was officially opened by Queen Victoria on 21 May 1894.

Summing up, Manchester was positioned in the vanguard of the new industrial age, with fundamental changes taking place at work, at home, and in public architecture. Out of the social conditions created by this upheaval, two classes emerged that came to dominate the political scene, both locally and nationally. The middle class prospered as the working class suffered, with some sections continuing to live in abject poverty at the turn of the century. Political ideas and many associations trace their roots to this period, but it is the relations between the emerging middle class and the more numerous working class that dominated the period and will be closely examined in the following chapters.

Notes

1. J.H. Clapham, 'The Factory System in 1815', *Economic Journal*, 1915, p.477.
2. R. Roberts, *A Ragged Schooling*, 1976, p.14.
3. V.A.C. Gatrell, 'Labour, Power and the Size of Firms in Lancashire Cotton in the Second Quarter of the Nineteenth Century', *Economic History Review*, 1977, p.95.
4. A. Kidd, *Manchester*, 1993, p.59.
5. J. Aiken, *A Description of Manchester*, 1795, p.32.
6. C. Hadfield and G. Biddle, *Canals in North West England*, 1970, p.285.
7. H. Perkin, *The Origins of Modern Society*, 1969, p.99.
8. *Manchester City News*, 14 April 1902.
9. K. Warrender, *Below Manchester*, 2009, p.133.
10. J. Kay, *The Moral and Physical Condition of the Working Classes*, 1832.
11. A.B. Reach, *Manchester and the Textile Districts in 1849*, 1849.
12. J. Roberts, *Working Class Housing in Nineteenth Century Manchester*, 1982.
13. C. Aspin, *Lancashire: The First Industrial Society*, 1969, p.62.
14. W. Cooke-Taylor, *Notes of a Tour of the Manufacturing Districts of Lancashire*, 1842, p.15.
15. J. Black and D.M. Macraild, *Nineteenth-Century Britain*, 2003, p.42.
16. Enclosure Acts 1760–1830.
17. A. Redford, *Labour Migration in England*, 1964, p.183.
18. J.K. Walton, *Lancashire*, 1987, p. 253.
19. E.H. Hunt, *Regional Wage Variations*, 1973, p.68.

20. J.G. Williamson, 'The Impact of the Irish on British Labour Markets During the Industrial Revolution', *Journal of Economic History*, 46, 1986, pp.693–720.

21. J. and B. Hammond, *The Town Labourer, 1760–1832*, 1917.

22. J. Whitaker, *A History of Manchester*, 1789.

23. P. Deane, *The First Industrial Revolution*, 1965, p.4.

24. J. and B. Hammond, *The Town Labourer, 1760–1832*, 1917.

25. 'Minutes of the Committee on Artizans and Machinery', 1824, p.113.

26. C. Aspin, *Lancashire: The First Industrial Society*, 1969, p.86.

27. Ibid.

28. C. Matthew, *The Nineteenth Century*, 2001, p.55.

29. R.N.W. Blake, *Disraeli*, 1969, pp.37–9.

30. J.K. Walton, *Lancashire*, 1987, p. 285.

31. J. Caminada, *Twenty-Five Years of Detective Life*, 1895.

32. M. Stedman, *Manchester Pals*, 1994, p.13.

33. J.K. Walton, *Lancashire*, 1987, p.226.

2

THE DEMISE OF THE WATCHMAN AND THE RISE OF JOSEPH NADIN, DEPUTY CONSTABLE

The chaotic state of Manchester at the beginning of the nineteenth century was described in the following manner by Mr and Mrs Webb:

> There were absolutely no building regulations. Each man put up his house where and as he chose, without regard for building line, width of street or access to light and air. Every householder encroached on the thoroughfare by overhanging windows, swinging signs, doors opening outwards, cellar flaps habitually open and mounting steps. The narrow ways for foot and wheeled traffic were uneven, unpaved and full of holes in which water and garbage accumulated, in places even a yard deep. There were, of course, no sewers and no water closets; except in the better parts, these were neither ash pits, nor privies, nor any similar conveniences. Pigs roamed about the streets – the only scavengers. At night, where there was no moon, the streets were in pitch darkness, except for an occasional lantern swinging over the door of a shopkeeper or rich householder. With this obstruction, dirt and darkness, it was perhaps a minor matter that there was no police.[1]

In short, under the rule of the Court Leet, Manchester's public services were either non-existent or grossly inefficient, at the same time as its population, industry and commerce were growing at an alarming rate. As the town developed, so its inhabitants increasingly made demands upon those in authority for this outmoded system to be reformed; they were met with indifference and then outright opposition.

Throughout the seventeenth and eighteenth centuries, justice and law enforcement was carried out by officers of the Court Leet, which was a hybrid court descended on the one side from the half-yearly sessions of the medieval court baron and on the other from the old Portmoot, which met four times a year to transact business relating to the town and its burgesses.

The background to manorial tenancy and rule lies in the medieval organisation of the country after 1066, when all land belonged to the monarch, hence 'real estate' or 'royal estate'. The king rewarded his loyal barons by giving some lands into their charge on condition that they would continue to provide him with military service in times of need. By the sixteenth century, Manchester's Lord of the Manor was Sir Oswald Mosley, who resided at Ancoats Hall in Every Street. Transfers of land and allegations of criminal acts were dealt with first in the baronial court and later in the 'little court' or Court Leet.

There were two market places in the centre of the town and between them stood the sessions house where the Court Leet met. Although manorial in form, the Court Leet's jurors were all burgesses, and the numerous officers appointed were also all burgesses. Of these officers, most were unpaid, but some of the inferior officers performing menial tasks received fees and perquisites.

Of the unpaid officers, the first to be elected by his fellow burgesses was always the boroughreeve, who was the chief officer of the town and most closely resembled the mayor of a borough. By the seventeenth century, this office had become honorary rather than active. Some of his duties were now being performed by the catchpole or bailiff, who was known as his deputy.

The most important executive functions of local administration were performed by the two constables who, like the boroughreeve, were appointed annually and were unpaid. The constables were responsible for the protection of the town by night and had the authority to summon a townsman to serve as a night watchman in his turn, or send a sufficient substitute. In practice, this came to mean the employment of privately paid watchmen, and this led to the direct employment of regular watchmen.

In 1750, Henry Fielding, Metropolitan magistrate, described watchmen employed in London as being:

> … chosen out of those poor, old, decrepit people who are, from their want of bodily strength, rendered incapable of getting a livelihood by work. These men, armed only with a pole, which some of them are scarcely able to lift, are to secure the persons and houses of His Majesty's subjects from the attacks of gangs of young, bold, stout, desperate and well-armed villains.

Manchester's watchmen found themselves equally ridiculed and subjected to severe criticism from the townspeople. In 1578, records show the jury of the Court Leet complaining about the negligence and dishonesty of those 'wicked watchmen who have been hired or rather bribed with money'. The jury issued an order to prevent further abuses, warning the constables that they should 'take none to the watch but such as are known to be honest, discreet and sober men, being able to yield account of the living, favourers to virtue and enemies to vice, no persons of misbehaviour, no suspected persons, no persons heretofore with bribes corrupted, nor any such like'. [2]

Apparently this warning was not heeded, because in 1610 the jury ordered that if any person appointed to serve as a watchman sent an insufficient person as his substitute, the offender would be compelled to serve in person or else pay a fine of 6s 8d. From this it was just a short step to the engagement of public watchmen paid out of local rates.

The period of watching varied slightly from year to year, but there was a general tendency to employ the night watchmen from 'Martinmas to Candlemas', that is during midwinter, from 11 November until 2 February. It had long been customary to provide candles for their lanterns 'in the dark nights when it was not moonshine'. [3] In 1653, the constables were ordered to provide also 'a hand-bell, which said bell shall every night be carried and used by the watch, who shall at every hour's end in their walking about the town give notice to the inhabitants of their vigilance by ringing the bell'.

The watchmen's rounds were regulated according to a set routine. Every evening before going on their rounds, all the watchmen were to assemble at the King Street office to be inspected as to their cleanliness, sobriety and general fitness for duty. They then reported to their respective corporals to be issued with a lantern, rick or rattle and a padlock, before going out on their beats. Six lock-ups were built for the immediate detention of prisoners, mostly drunks, vagrants and juveniles. These were located at King Street, in the old town hall; Swan Street, Shudehill; Kirby Street, Ancoats; Deansgate; London Road; and Oldham Road.

Lanterns were an essential piece of equipment by the late eighteenth century, as the streets of Manchester were illuminated solely by two oil lamps, one on the old bridge across the Irwell and the other at the Manchester Cross. It was not until 1807 that the very first gas lamp was illuminated above the police office in Police Street, off Deansgate. By 1826, 4¾ miles of streets had been illuminated by gas lamps, installed by the Police Commissioners.

The issuing of padlocks served to enable the watchmen to secure premises that were found insecure during the night. Should a watchman find it necessary to get in touch with other watchmen, he would 'spring his rick' to attract attention. Also, he was expected to reassure the townspeople that all was well, and in the early hours he would perform a social service by waking up workers for the 6 a.m. start of their shift. This practice was frowned upon by the town's new Police Commissioner when he arrived in 1839, but he had to concede that the benefits outweighed the 'inappropriateness' of such practices.

By 1815, fifty-three watchmen were employed, each working a ten-hour shift starting at 8 p.m. and ending around 6 a.m. the following morning. During the next ten years, the number of watchmen had increased to seventy-four and their wages varied between 13*s* and 18*s* per week. By this time, the night watch contained three recognisable ranks – constable, corporal and sergeant – with each watchman being issued a personalised number for identification. Theirs was a thankless task; they were subjected to vile abuse from the community at large, attacked and beaten up, with little compensation or remuneration at the week's end. Often as not they retreated to their boxes after midnight, turning out occasionally to call out the time of the hour if they happened to be awake.

Assisting the constables and watchmen was the Beadle, who was a paid officer of the Court Leet. As a perquisite to his wages he received 4*d* for every 'rogue' he whipped. Considering that in just one year it was reported that he carried out seventy-four whippings, his remuneration was quite significant. He was provided with a uniform made up of 'a good cloth coat laced with yellow kersey, together with a hat, a whip and an official staff with a knob on it'.

The office of Beadle in its early days appears to have been intermittent and casual. Unable or unwilling to commit themselves to the many onerous tasks demanded of them, the constables decided, in addition to the Beadle, they would appoint a full-time paid deputy on a salary of £10, as well as the occasional fees and expenses, which soon amounted to several times his salary.

There was an embarrassing variety of functions to perform or at least to supervise. Not only were the constables responsible for the regular payment of wages and salaries to their staff, but they had to make a continual stream of disbursements, large and small, for such miscellaneous services as 'beating the drum for two days at the General Muster; walking the town two days at Whitsuntide; punishing Margaret Buckley for troubling market folk in the meal house; conveying out of town one James Smith, a leper; watching the town when the Cheshire soldiers were here for two nights'. There were also 'rogues, sturdy beggars and vagabonds to be whipped, relieved and sent out of town; scolding women to be ducked in the pond; plague victims to be isolated in the Collyhurst cabins'. Each of these occasions warranted a separate entry in the *Constable's Accounts* book, including the actual sums of money spent on each.[4]

In the second half of the eighteenth century, the professional standing of the office of the Deputy Constable was to rise considerably, along with his salary. In 1750, his salary was raised from £10 to £20; in 1778, it was raised to £80; in 1786 it went up to £150, where it remained for the next nineteen years.

The constables found it extremely difficult to recruit the type of man who would perform the duties of Deputy Constable to their satisfaction and not succumb to the many temptations available. Richard Unite was appointed to the post in 1792 and went on to attract criticism almost from the outset. He was alleged to have feathered his own nest by charging innkeepers for the favour of billeting soldiers, blackmailing vulnerable litigants, taking 'hush money', and, as a special favour to distraught husbands, often he would lock up a troublesome wife and certify her as a lunatic in return for a 'generous donation'.[5]

His reign did not last long. A Committee of Inquiry, conducted by irate ratepayers stung into action by a rise in the local rates, revealed the corrupt practices carried out by the full-time official and he was dismissed immediately. His successor was Thomas Slack, who had previously kept a grocer's shop at the top of Market Street. Sadly for all concerned, Slack was drowned at Liverpool Docks only weeks after his appointment in 1797.

In the meantime, the Court Leet became aware that Richard Unite was expressing an interest in returning to his old position, and they were determined to block him in any such attempt. In advertising the vacant post, it was specified:

> No person need apply whose character will not stand the strictest scrutiny.
> To prevent any misunderstanding, Richard Unite, who in an advertisement
> in Mr. Wheeler's paper on Saturday last, called himself the deputy constable,
> has not been appointed to that office.[6]

Eventually, the position went to William Waters, about whom little is known, but who apparently held the office without scandal for five years until his retirement in 1802.

He was succeeded by Joseph Nadin. Like his predecessors, Nadin had plenty of opportunities to unlawfully feather his own nest, as was the custom of the time, but there is no reliable evidence that this was the case and there is no doubt that the Court Leet and Manchester's ratepayers valued his services highly during the next twenty years; so much so, that they increased his salary with some rapidity. His starting salary in 1802 was £150. By 1805, it had gone up to £200, in 1807 to £300, and then to £350 by 1810. By comparison, the average salary of a Manchester tradesman at this time was between £20 and £30.[7]

Nadin was appointed on the recommendation of the Manchester Society for the Prosecution of Felons, which had been founded in 1787 by a group of Manchester tradesman, manufacturers and dyers 'for the protection of property and for the successful prosecution of thieves and receivers'. A fund was set aside 'for the purpose of defraying any expenses incurred'.

Nadin had come to their attention whilst he was working as a mill manager in Stockport. His factory and some of its machinery had been damaged by 'plug plot' rioters who had been protesting at the installation of modern machinery. He had successfully prosecuted those responsible for committing damage in his factory and, at the request of other factory owners and managers, successfully prosecuted others who had committed damage and theft at neighbouring factories.

Soon after his appointment as Deputy Constable, Nadin introduced a regime that demanded strict adherence to the rules and procedures he set down for the efficient running of the Court Leet's police. His efforts soon came to be recognised by the newly founded Police Commissioners, who had been given statutory authority for the night police (the Court Leet now being responsible only for the day police). At a meeting of the Police Commissioners held on 16 August 1805, discussions took place about the favourable impression Nadin had made since his appointment. They concluded: 'Thanks to Mr Nadin, after just twelve months, complaints about the slackness and laziness of police/watchmen on night-time duties has ceased abruptly.'[8]

The Commissioners decided to approach the Court Leet with a proposition that Nadin take over the superintendence of the night watch as well as the day police. The Court Leet agreed and Nadin was invited to take over all of the 'police business' in the town. The existing superintendent of the night watch, James Horsefield, was transferred to the Scavenging Department, with responsibility for waste collection and disposal. From this time on, Joseph Nadin became the top police official in Manchester, a position acknowledged and endorsed by both official bodies in the town.

In February 1818, Joseph Nadin came under personal attack from Mr George Teale, a Manchester solicitor representing two boys who had been arrested by a special constable named Hindley. It was alleged that the two boys, named Hill and Lear, were found in possession of stolen goods after being entrapped by the special constable, who was acting on the instructions of Joseph Nadin.

The solicitor further alleged that throughout the proceedings, the special constable was being instructed what to do and say by the Deputy Constable.

At the end of the hearing, the magistrates dismissed the charge against the two boys, recommending that the boroughreeve dismiss Special Constable Hindley, and then announced that all of the evidence they had heard pointed to fabrication on the part of the special constable, who was acting alone, and not under any instruction.[9]

Having been cleared of any wrongdoing, Joseph Nadin went on the offensive and instituted proceedings against Mr Teale to recover 'penalties' of £4,600, with costs. Nadin won the case and was awarded the full amount sought in damages and costs, which effectively ruined Mr Teale, both professionally and financially. It also provided Nadin with a substantial sum of money that, together with his improved salary and perquisites, made him a wealthy man.

Moved by these allegations of corruption, the boroughreeves and constables of Manchester published the following letter of support in the *Manchester Gazette*, dated 4 July 1818:

We the undersigned, being all persons who have served the offices of boroughreeve and constable from the time of Mr. Nadin's appointment as deputy constable, now surviving and residing in Manchester and its surrounding neighbourhood, felt ourselves called upon at a time when the police of the town, and the character of Mr. Nadin in particular, have been wantonly and maliciously aspersed, to declare that we have always had the fullest reason to be satisfied with his integrity and fidelity as well as with his zeal and ability on the execution of his duties of his office.

And we each for ourselves further certify, that the whole of the rewards awarded to the township of Manchester upon convictions in cases of burglary, highway robbery, cow stealing, horse stealing and sheep stealing (the only cases in which they are allowed) and the proceeds of the several Tyburn Tickets sold in our respective years in office (except the 15 per cent allowed to the deputy constable) have been regularly brought to the credit of the town, before as well as since 1810, when a resolution making a distinct provision for this purpose, was passed at the parish table.

We also certify that during our respective years of office, a book has been kept in which all stolen property has been regularly entered and duly accounted for, and that the proceeds from the sale of unclaimed stolen property, from the time of Mr. Nadin's first appointment in the year 1802, has been regularly placed to the credit of the town. Signed:

1802 Richard Wilson
     John Mather
1803 James Herbert
     Richard Rushforth
1804 William Fox
     Joseph Seddon
1805 Richard Entwistle
     John Ratcliffe
1806 William Starkie
     Richard Wood
1807 Thomas Belcher
     Samuel Phillips
1808 Thomas Fosbroke
     Jeremiah Fielding
1809 John Touchett
1810 Thomas Hardman
     William Garnett
1811 H. Birley
     Joseph Winter
1812 Edward Lloyd
     James Kersley
1813 William Edenson
     Gilbert Winter
1814 F.S. Potter
     John Touchett
1815 Thomas Williams
1816 William Mitchell
     B. Bright
1817 Nathaniel Wainhouse
     T.S. Withington
1818 Thomas Salter
     William Sandford

Notwithstanding this testimony and support, Nadin's reputation continued to be sullied by Manchester's radicals, who appear to have placed great reliance on gossip and rumour in preference to more reliable sources of information. Fletcher Moss, for example, in his *Chronicles of Cheadle* (1894), provides a description of Nadin that is laced with vitriol:

Nadin had gone to Manchester barefoot and barelegged with nothing but a beefy body. He got the reputation of having had lots of innocent men hanged. Six different men have told me that, although they do not give particular instances. In these tales of bygone generations, it is very interesting to notice how often wrong men got hanged. This notorious constable died at last but no-one seems to know what became of him or his body.[10]

Nadin's biggest critic was Manchester newspaper editor Archibald Prentice, who arrived in Manchester from Scotland in 1815 and assisted John Edward Taylor in setting up the *Manchester Guardian*. Prentice wrote:

> For more than ten years this coarse man has been the real ruler of Manchester under a succession of municipal officers and magistrates, who thought they exercised a wholesome authority, when at his suggestion, they sought to repress by every means of coercion the rising demand for political and social rights.[11]

Nadin, of course, was the public face of the Tory administration in Manchester, to which Prentice was fiercely opposed. It would seem, however, that Nadin was not alone in attracting the wrath of Prentice. First of all, he had a fall-out with his friend John Taylor after he criticised him publicly for being too cautious and moderate; then there was Richard Cobden, one of the leaders of the Anti-Corn Law League, who reported that he had to restrain Prentice when he was pressing Peel for greater concessions over the Corn Laws; local Chartist leaders were also at odds with Prentice over his claim that their tactics were too moderate; in his *Political Register*, William Cobbett described Prentice as a 'prig' and in the *Manchester Advertiser*, Prentice was described as 'the most noisy in self-applause of all reformers'.[12]

Critics of Nadin often refer to his practice of 'making every offence a felony so that he would qualify for a reward'.[13] What they have overlooked is that only robbery, burglary and animal stealing were worth a reward at this time, and, as noted by Nadin's supporters, his employers encouraged this practice as it benefited the ratepayers far more than it did the Deputy Constable.[14] (Nadin would receive only 15 per cent of the value of a reward, the rest going to his employers to benefit the town.) In 1819, the law was changed so that rewards by the courts (known as Tyburn Tickets) following successful prosecutions were no longer fixed but were only to be made at the discretion of the trial judge.

Tyburn Tickets were parliament-sanctioned, and were presented by the court to a person who had successfully brought a prosecution ending with the execution of the offender at the notorious Tyburn prison in West London. Armed with this document, the prosecutor could not only claim exemption from any unwelcome public duties but could exchange the ticket for a sum of money. This practice of rewarding prosecutors soon spread nationwide, and was considered appropriate for defraying prosecution expenses that may have been incurred in bringing witnesses to court.

A more reliable source of information about Deputy Constable Joseph Nadin can be found in the writings of the Middleton-born poet Samuel Bamford, who was present on St Peter's Field at the Peterloo Massacre and, most significantly, was actually arrested by Nadin on two separate occasions. In his biographical notes, Bamford wrote:

> The date was the 29th March, 1817. I was walking towards the churchyard, when [a] voice hallooed and looking back I beheld Joseph Scott, the deputy constable of Middleton, hastening towards me. I concluded instantly that he wanted me; and disdaining the thought of flying I returned and met him, and he took hold of me, saying I was the King's prisoner. I asked him what for and he said I should see presently, and we had not gone many yards on our return when we were met by Mr. Nadin, the deputy constable of Manchester and about six or eight special constables all well armed with staves, pistols and blunderbusses. Nadin was I suppose about 6 feet 1 inch tall, with an uncommon breadth and solidarity of frame. He was also strongly built, upright in gait and active in motion. His head was full sized, his complexion sallow, his hair dark and slightly grey; his features were broad and non-intellectual, his voice loud, his language coarse and illiterate, and his manner rude and overbearing to equals and inferiors. He was represented as being exceedingly crafty in his business, and somewhat unfeeling withal, but I have never heard and certainly never knew that he maltreated his prisoners. At times he would indulge in a raillery with them possibly for a reason of his own but I never was led to suppose that he threw away a word of consolement on these occasions. He was certainly a somewhat remarkable person in uncommon times, and acting in an arduous situation. He showed, however, that he had the homely tact to take care of his own interests. He housed a good harvest whilst his sun was up and retired to spend his evening in ease and plenty on a farm of his own within the borders of Cheshire.[15]

Bamford had many opportunities to blacken the name of Nadin but chose not to do so. His description of Nadin being 'a remarkable person in uncommon times' appears to sum him up quite well. Even Prentice grudgingly acknowledged that Bamford 'would seem to have had no dislike to the rough deputy constable'.[16] Undoubtedly, Nadin was a controversial figure, but for him to be dismissed as a 'corrupt and brutal official' would seem to fly in the face of testimony provided by office-holders and contemporaries. Nadin was no saint, far from it, but in the context of a volatile and dangerous early nineteenth-century Manchester, he showed resilience and courage in the face of personal and often politically motivated hostility.

In 1822, Nadin retired to his Manchester home in Lloyd Street, Greenheys, before returning to his roots in Cheshire after acquiring Orrishmere Farm, Cheadle. He died on 20 March 1848, and was buried in St James' Cemetery, Charlotte Street, Manchester, where he had spent twenty years as a church-warden. He was survived by his two sons, Thomas and Joseph Nadin, who practised as solicitors in offices adjoining the Queen's Theatre in Quay Street, at its junction with Peter Street. It is understood that Joseph Nadin (jnr) was the theatre owner.[17]

Nadin was succeeded by a former Bow Street Runner named Joseph Lavender, who took up residence in a house in King Street, on a site where the Bank of England now stands. Lavender's staff consisted of four Beadles, whose names were Thomas Worthington, George Moss, Anthony Jefferson and John Page. There were also seven assistants and four street keepers, and 200 special constables, to be called upon 'in extraordinary circumstances'.

In his *Reminiscences of Manchester*, writer J.T. Slugg describes an encounter with Lavender and his staff when they faced an angry mob in Ancoats:

> The colour of their livery was brown. I well remember hearing of a riot in the neighbourhood of Ancoats, when one or two factories were set on fire. I was passing the Royal Hotel just as Lavender was coming up Mosley Street at the head of about nine or ten beadles [the writer may have mistaken assistants for beadles] walking in a single line, each carrying a drawn cutlass in his hand, and I remember seeing them cross over Mosley Street. They were assisted in quelling the disturbance by a number of special constables from the Ancoats district.[18]

In the following chapter we have another opportunity to look at Joseph Nadin's conduct, when evaluating the available evidence surrounding the historic event known as the Peterloo Massacre.

Notes

1. S. and B. Webb, *Statutory Authorities for Special Purposes*, 1922, p.236.
2. Court Leet Records, Vol. 1, p.195.
3. *Constable's Accounts*, Vol. 1, p.262.
4. *Constable's Accounts*, Vol. 3, p.132.
5. S. and B. Webb, *The Parish and the County*, 1906.
6. Court Leet Records, Vol. 9, pp.132, 184.
7. A. Briggs, *Victorian Cities*, 1963, p.209.
8. Proceedings of Manchester's Police Commissioners, Vol. 1, 16 August 1805.
9. L.S. Marshall, *Development of Public Opinion in Manchester 1780–1820*, 1946, p.93.
10. F. Moss, *Chronicles of Cheadle*, 1894, p.174.
11. A. Prentice, *Historical Sketches and Personal Recollections*, 1851, p.34.
12. P. Ziegler, *National Biography.*
13. See HO papers 42.153.1816.
14. Statement published by the Manchester Society on its disbandment, June 1848.
15. S. Bamford, *Passages in the Life of a Radical*, 1839, p.84.
16. A. Prentice, *Historical Sketches and Personal Recollections*, 1851, p.98.
17. *City News*, 15 April 1893.
18. J.T. Slugg, *Reminiscences of Manchester*, 1848, p.236.

3

PETERLOO

With no effective representative voice in parliament, the angry, hungry and cyclically unemployed poor turned to populist orators and pamphleteers like Henry Hunt and William Cobbett for ideas on the best way forward. While Cobbett advocated parliamentary reform through his newspaper the *Political Register*, Hunt employed his oratory skills at public gatherings across the country, sometimes ending up in prison as a consequence. It came as no surprise, therefore, that Henry Hunt was invited to be the guest speaker at a public meeting to be held on 16 August 1819, on St Peter's Field, in the centre of Manchester.

Both men were fired by the radical egalitarian ideas of Thomas Paine, published in *The Rights of Man*, which centred on a redistribution of parliamentary seats, secret ballots and universal manhood suffrage.

In the years leading up to Peterloo, the labour force in and around Manchester was continually involved in economic struggle, manifested in public protests and widespread disruption. Faced with cyclical unemployment, economic slumps, high food prices and repressive labour laws, many workers targeted the factories that housed the 'animal machines', perceived as being the principal cause of their distress. In the vanguard of this Luddite movement were the domestic handloom weavers, whose livelihoods were being undermined by the modernisation of the manufacturing process and by a labour market packed with migrant rural workers and demobbed soldiers, eager to try their hand at handloom weaving, which was not considered a highly skilled craft. Dr Kay, Medical Officer of Health in Manchester, wrote in 1832:

Whilst the engine runs, the people must work (men, women and children) yoked together with iron and steam. The animal machines, breakable in the best case, subject to a thousand sources of suffering, chained fast to the iron machine, which knows no suffering and no weariness. [1]

At one extreme, mass protests against symbols of oppression were seen as part of the development of a working-class consciousness by Marxist historians such as E.P. Thompson, who wrote: 'Luddism was a quasi-insurrectionary movement which continually trembled on the edge of ulterior revolutionary objectives.' [2] Dismissing such claims, Malcolm Thomis and Peter Holt maintained that the Luddite movement 'was more a spasm in the death throes of declining trades than the birth pangs of revolution'. [3]

A great deal of documentary evidence about the Luddites' political motivation is drawn from Home Office reports, information specifically obtained from local spies employed by office-holders, such as the local magistrates. Thompson took the view that such evidence could be taken at face value, but it is important to recognise that these accounts from paid spies should be treated with caution. Quite often it was in the financial interest of the spies themselves to embellish their stories, in expectation of attracting a greater remuneration. Indeed, spies were very well paid for their stories, as can be seen from a report from Bolton indicating that a local spy was paid £9 5s and £17 2s for reports delivered to the magistrates between July and December 1805. By comparison, a Bolton weaver was being paid 12s per week, working in excess of twelve hours a day.

In December 1816, alarmed at the volatile situation in Manchester, Home Secretary Addington wrote to Rev. Ethelston, Justice of the Peace in Manchester:

As it appears to be your decided opinion that Fleming and Campbell might be usefully employed as secret agents to obtain further intelligence of plans and movements of the disaffected, there can be no objection to make weekly remunerations to them, on a modest scale, as you may consider sufficient for their trouble. [4]

In comparison with other textile workers, domestic handloom weavers were by the very nature of their work and lives disorganised and isolated, often residing in small hamlets or townships across Lancashire and the West Riding of Yorkshire. Bythell points to the isolation of handloom weavers as being a basic weakness, which prompted them to resort to such desperate, extraordinary methods of voicing their grievances through the Luddite movement. [5]

At the end of the eighteenth century, work was booming for this group of workers, and high earnings characterised the craft, attracting many workers from farms and rural occupations. In the wider Manchester area, work was 'put out' to domestic weavers at the start of the week and then the finished work was collected at the end of the week, often by representatives of large-scale manufacturers. One such example was the firm of Peel and Yates of Bury, which employed thousands of weavers across Lancashire.[6]

The trade was exposed to the most violent fluctuations, however, which created a vulnerable, exposed workforce. At its peak in 1805, it is estimated that one in six of the population of Lancashire was dependent on handloom weaving, either as a full-time or part-time occupation. In the years that followed the introduction of power loom weaving, the process of weaving cotton could be carried out at a much lower cost, whilst producing greater quantities of cotton, within the factories.

Recognising the sad and tragic decline of this group of workers, the Select Committee on Handloom Weavers wrote: 'The sufferings of that large and valuable body have for years continued to an extent and intensity scarcely to be credited or conceived and have been borne with a degree of patience unexampled.'[7]

To fully appreciate the direct action of the Luddites, account must be taken of the appalling conditions in which domestic weavers were having to live. An illuminating statement issued by a group of weavers in Bolton, dated 27 February 1826, reads: 'A good weaver who formerly earned from 6 shillings a day, cannot now earn 6 shillings a week working a sixteen hour day. Many weavers are now on half work and earning 3 shillings.' According to G.H. Wood's detailed analysis, entitled 'The estimates of the average weekly wages in the cotton trade in Lancashire', the weavers earned 18s a week in 1801, but by 1830 their earnings had fallen to just 6s.

At the same time as protesting against the introduction of new technology in the textile factories, the Luddites were also worried that their handicraft skills were being eroded as a result of what they regarded as the poorer-quality of clothing being produced in the factories and by the influx of unskilled demobbed soldiers in search of casual work. Their attacks on factories were a form of protest that created fear among employers and the government, but they were essentially reactionary and economic in character rather than political. Whilst they had some limited political concerns, these were never developed to the extent described in the reports of Home Office spies. The Luddites were far from being simple-minded opponents of technology, as they have been popularly portrayed. In an era when the

Combination Acts prohibited organised trade unionism, they resorted to acts of criminal damage as a means of highlighting their grievances and pressuring factory owners into providing them with more work instead of taking it from them. Although they lacked any real political force, those in power did not see it that way and applied the full weight of the law whenever individuals described as Luddites appeared at court. In one case held at York Assizes in 1813, seventeen Luddites were convicted of arson at a West Yorkshire factory and sentenced to be hanged.

Machine breaking was not the only manifestation of workers' frustration and anger in the first quarter of the nineteenth century. In and around Manchester, demonstrations would often spill over into violent confrontations with the police and the military. Baines records one such gathering, which took place in the year 1808:

> Manchester was much agitated by a contest between weavers and their employers, regarding the rate of wages being paid, and the interference of parliament was sought by the former, to protect their interests. In the meantime, the weavers assembled on Tuesday, 24 May, and again the following day, in St George's Fields, in large bodies, and in a manner which awakened the apprehensions of the authorities in the town. At the latter of these meetings, the Riot Act was read and the military were afterwards called out by the magistrates to disperse the assembly; in the discharge of which service one of the weavers was killed, and several of them wounded. But the circumstances which distinguished the events of this day was the appearance upon the field of Lt. Col. Joseph Hanson of Strangeways Hall, mounted on his charger. On his arrival, Mr Hanson addressed the gathering in a speech, which afterwards became the subject of judicial inquiry at the Assizes at Lancaster and Mr Hanson, after being found guilty of aiding and abetting the rioters, was sentenced by the court to pay a fine of £100 and to be imprisoned for six months in the custody of the Marshall at the Marshalsea Court.[8]

Strangeways Hall, the home of Lt-Col Hanson, became the site of a new prison building a few years later.

What would often start out as a food riot or an attack on a factory, ended with bloodshed and fatalities. Writing in a local newspaper, Prentice described a food riot that occurred on 21 April 1812, in Oldham Road, New Cross, when a cart carrying food to the market at Shudehill was stopped by locals and its load carried off:

Shops in the vicinity were also attacked and their contents looted. Eventually the mob was dispersed by the local militia but only as far as neighbouring Middleton. There they met up with a group of weavers, miners and out of work factory workers, who had been protesting against the introduction of power looms at the weaving mills of Burton and Son.

The crowd swelled to around 2,000 strong. The internal part of the factory being guarded, a musket was discharged in the hope of intimidating and dispersing the assailants but it was found ineffectual, the throwing of stones continuing, and after the expiration of about fifteen minutes, firing of ball commenced from the soldiers in the factory. In a very short space of time the effects were all too shockingly seen in the death of three and, it is said, about ten wounded. Here this horrid conflict terminated for that night, which was spent in dreadful preparation.

The morning brought with it great apprehension, the insurgents gathered, many of them armed with guns and scythes tied to the ends of poles, the factory was protected by soldiers, so strongly as to be impregnable; they then flew to the house of Mr Burton where they wreaked their vengeance by setting it on fire. A party of soldiers, horse and foot, from Manchester, pursued these misguided people, some of whom made a feeble stand, but here again death was the consequence, five of them being shot and many more wounded.[9]

The same event was witnessed by Samuel Bamford, who wrote:

> The mob, it should be understood, was on this day armed with guns, scythes and old swords. The houses of Mr. Emanuel Burton at Parkfield and Mr. Burton senior at Rhodes, were ransacked before being set alight. The Scots Greys arrived and dispersed the mob speedily and effectually. Shots were fired from both sides and prisoners taken.[10]

Two weeks later the political establishment was rocked by the assassination of the prime minister, Mr Spencer Perceval, at a London theatre. He was shot at close range by a lone gunman who was suffering from a mental illness. News of his death reverberated throughout the political class and created a brief period of crisis, especially as it took place in the midst of reports of disturbances and social unrest in the North West of England.

The period 1815–19 was critical for the working class on at least two levels. First, severe economic depression set in and threw thousands out of work, and second, parliament passed the Corn Laws in 1815, which protected growers from the vagaries of the free market by excluding foreign wheat until its price reached 80s, 'a famine price'. Manchester, like most manufacturing towns, felt the impoverishing effects of this protectionist legislation more than most. The population not only had to endure the high price of bread, but also the additional strains on the labour market brought about by yet another economic depression.

In response to this latest situation, a group of Manchester's starving working men set out on 10 March 1817, to march peacefully to London to hand in a petition to the Prince Regent, pleading for his intervention. The marchers were to become known as the 'blanketeers', simply because so many of them were wrapped in blankets to keep out the cold winds. They set out from Manchester and reached Lancashire Hill, near Stockport, before being dispersed by a body of yeomanry who had followed them along the route. A total of 167 marchers were taken into custody, many of them having sustained sabre wounds, and one marcher was shot and killed. Describing the blanketeers as they set out from Manchester, Samuel Bamford wrote:

> Some of them formed a straggly line in Mosley Street and marched along Piccadilly, being continually joined by others, until the whole body was collected near Ardwick Green. The appearance of these misdirected people was calculated to excite, in the considerate minds, pity rather than resentment. A body of Yeomanry was seen soon afterwards following these simple-minded men.[11]

One man who helped to shape the ideas and future actions of the working class at this critical time was William Cobbett. Through the pages of his newspaper, the *Political Register*, Cobbett turned the workers away from direct action and towards more 'peaceful resistance', with the ultimate aim of securing a reform of parliament. His influence was well recognised at the Home Office, which was inundated with reports from their paid spies. 'Cobbett has done more with his twopenny papers than any thousand beside him, as anyone can get their hands on them the price being so low.'[12]

Samuel Bamford agreed:

> At this time, the writings of William Cobbett suddenly became the great authority, they were read on nearly every cottage hearth in the manufacturing districts of South Lancashire and those of Leicester, Derby and Nottinghamshire; also in many of the Scottish manufacturing districts. Their influence was speedily visible, he directed his readers to the true cause

of their sufferings –misgovernment and its proper corrective – parliamentary reform. Riots soon became scarce. Instead of riots, Hampden Clubs were now established in many of our towns and the villages that surround.[13]

Strenuous efforts were made by the authorities to stop the *Register* from being sold and read by or to the working class. The government's message was expressed in *The Times* newspaper on 3 January 1817:

> It is a great evil of the present day that such is the poverty of the more humble classes of the community so that if they do read, or know anything of public affairs, it must be in the cheaper forms, and hence they become the dupes, to a great extent, of the basest and most profligate of men.

Cobbett and his salesmen were frequently arrested, fined and even sentenced to imprisonment. A Warrington bookseller, whose house was found to contain copies of the *Register*, was imprisoned, while two men from Shropshire were arrested under the Vagrancy Act for selling the *Register* and were ordered to be flogged at the whipping post. Cobbett himself spent time in prison, and for a time in 1819 went to America with his wife to avoid the authorities.

While Cobbett was busily advocating reform in print, his friend Henry Hunt was addressing crowds across the country, preaching the same message. These gatherings alarmed the government as much as Cobbett's *Register* and, being well aware of the sensitivity aroused, Hunt became especially careful not to incite or lead on the crowds who came to listen. Notwithstanding his assurances that 'we want no tumults and no riots', violence did break out, on occasion, perpetrated by members of fringe groups using the cover of a peaceful assembly to engage the authorities.

One such meeting took place at Stockport in February 1819, when the local Union Society called for equal rights and parliamentary reform. A large crowd had gathered to hear a succession of speakers when violence erupted. The local magistrates became fearful and read the Riot Act. Some of those in attendance were wearing 'caps of liberty' as a tribute to the French revolutionaries, and this apparently annoyed the town's Deputy Constable Birch to the extent that he took it upon himself to remove a cap from the wearer's head. This action provoked a violent reaction from the crowd, which resulted in Mr Birch sustaining serious head injuries from which he later died.

In the weeks that followed there were a number of public meetings calling for a reform of parliament. At one meeting, held at St Peter's Field on 14 June, it was estimated that those assembled totalled 20,000. Other meetings were held at Ashton-under-Lyne, Oldham, Middleton, Royton, Lees and Bury. At the end of each meeting it was agreed that petitions be sent to the king and the Prince Regent, appealing for them to intervene in their disputes with masters and to support their demands for parliamentary reform.

Fearful magistrates urged the Home Secretary for greater powers to put down these gatherings, but their appeals, like those of the protestors, were rebuffed. On 1 July 1819, the magistrates sent the following letter to the Home Secretary:

> Urged on by the harangues of a few desperate demagogues we anticipate at no distant period a general rising and possessing no power to prevent the meetings which are weekly held, we as magistrates are at a loss how to stem the influence of the dangerous and seditious doctrines which are criminally disseminated.
> Signed, J. Norris, J. Sylvester, W. Marriott, R. Wright, C. W. Ethelston.

The temperature continued to rise, however, and on 23 July local magistrates held a meeting at the New Bayley courthouse, after which a proclamation was issued, which read:

> A very disturbed spirit is found in the manufacturing districts. Special Constables are to be appointed. Peaceful inhabitants should form voluntary associations under magistracy for action and should apply to the Lord Lieutenant for arms. A select committee of magistrates is to be formed.[14]

Under the Defence of the Realm Act 1798, each Lord Lieutenant was required to maintain a list of all able-bodied men aged 15–60, for the purpose of home defence. These volunteers formed infantry or cavalry units and were provided with arms. These units were in addition to the local volunteer corps and yeomanry set up under the Volunteer Act of 1794. Fearful of a French invasion at the time, the government had authorised the use of arms for the dual purposes of home defence and policing (Clause 31).

News of a proposed meeting to be held on 16 August prompted the magistrates to issue warning notices; these were placed around the town and read:

> Whereas it appears by an advertisement in the *Manchester Observer* paper of this day – 31.7.1819 – that a public and illegal meeting is convened for 16 August, to be held in the area near St. Peter's church; we the undersigned magistrates acting for the counties Palatine of Lancashire and Cheshire do

hereby caution all persons to abstain, at their peril, from attending such illegal meeting.

The organisers ignored this warning and went on to invite the famous orator, Henry Hunt, to address the meeting on the injustices of the parliamentary system. Hunt accepted their invitation, proclaiming, 'It is a grave injustice that Manchester has not a single representative in parliament.'

The reform movement, which Hunt and Cobbett represented, was not particularly intellectual, and it might be argued that it suffered as a consequence. But it did offer the most coherent political programme of the day. Under the banner headline of 'parliamentary reform', a ten-point plan was published:

1. Do away with corruption at elections.
2. Do away with parliamentary interest. People should succeed on merit rather than connection.
3. Do away with sinecures.
4. Enquire into and cut down on salaries.
5. Reduce the Army and sift the Navy.
6. Employ no secret service and no spies.
7. Reform the bar and make it independent.
8. Give real freedom to the press.
9. Cut down the civil list.
10. Stop paying interest on the national debt and reduce taxes.

In addition to this plan, the reformers advocated annual parliaments and secret ballots. Idealistic it may have been, but this reform movement attracted the support of many of Manchester's radicals, who tended to congregate around John Edward Taylor, John Shuttleworth and the Potter family. These cotton merchants, manufacturers and journalists were also in the leadership group that called for a reform of local government.

On the morning of 16 August 1819, marchers from the manufacturing districts in and around Manchester set out to attend the reform meeting on St Peter's Field in the centre of the town. According to the many handbills posted around the town, the meeting had been called 'to take into consideration the most speedy and effectual mode of obtaining radical reform in the Commons House of Parliament; and to consider the propriety of the unrepresented inhabitants of Manchester electing a person to represent them in Parliament'.

St Peter's Field was the traditional meeting place for workers for many miles around, its only exceptional characteristic being its size. According to Robert Reid, its broadest dimension was about 170yds in one direction and 150yds in the other. Down its eastern edge ran Mount Street, and Windmill Street ran the length of the south-western edge. From its northern edge stood the Quakers' Meeting-House and burial grounds. St Peter's Church stood outside the field, its front entrance approached by Peter Street.[15]

Local magistrates, under the leadership of chief magistrate Mr William Hulton, assembled at 11 a.m. in Mr Buxton's house, situated in Mount Street, overlooking the field and approximately 100yds from the spot where Hunt and his fellow speakers were to address the crowd. It was estimated that between 50,000 and 60,000 people assembled that day to listen to the speakers and to show their solidarity.[16]

Troops had been turned out early that morning, and were stationed at a number of key points in the town. The Manchester and Salford Yeomanry, made up of amateur soldiers, were off Portland Street and the regulars of the 15th Hussars and Cheshire Yeomanry were in St John Street. Other contingents of regular soldiers were stationed in Lower Mosley Street, Brazennose Street, and Dickenson Street. Between the magistrates and the hustings was a double line of special constables numbering around 300.

The officer commanding the Northern District of the army was General Sir John Byng, a veteran of Waterloo. He was absent on the morning of 16 August, having decided to accept an invitation to a race meeting at York and leaving his second in command, Lt-Col L'Estrange, in charge.

The assembled magistrates came under pressure from a delegation of some sixty tradesmen and merchants, who declared that they feared for their personal safety in view of the serious disruption that was likely to occur. After hearing the views of his fellow magistrates, Mr Hulton decided to issue and sign an arrest warrant, 'considering that the lives and properties of all persons in Manchester were in the greatest danger'.[17] The warrant contained the names of four men: Henry Hunt, John Knight, James Moorhouse and Joseph Johnson, who were all expected on the hustings.

Surveying the scene, the numbers gathering, and the state of agitation, Mr Hulton tasked fellow magistrate, Rev. Ethelston, with reading a proclamation from the Riot Act, and he did so by leaning out of a first-floor window in Mr Buxton's house. Under the terms of the Riot Act 1714, where twelve or more persons are riotously or unlawfully assembled to the disturbance of the public peace, a magistrate should read the following proclamation:

His Majesty the King chargeth and commandeth all persons, being assembled, immediately to disperse themselves and peacefully to depart to their habitations or to their lawful business, upon the pains contained in the Act made in the first year of King George, for preventing tumults and riotous assemblies. God save the King.

Anyone who remained on the scene after one hour from the time the proclamation was read became liable to arrest under the Act.

Joseph Nadin, as the Deputy Constable, took possession of the arrest warrant and went to the field with a group of special constables. However, he returned to the magistrates soon after to declare that the 300 special constables at his disposal were not a sufficient force to enable him to execute the warrant.

At this point, messages were sent to Portland Street, where the yeomanry was stationed, and to St John Street, where the hussars and Cheshire Yeomanry were stationed, calling on the military to attend and support the Deputy Constable in executing the warrant. The first to respond was the yeomanry, who made their way into the crowd and opened up a pathway sufficient for Nadin and his special constables to safely walk through to the hustings and make their arrests. As it turned out, Knight and Moorhouse were no longer on the scene and so Hunt and Johnson climbed down from the wooden cart used as hustings and were taken into custody. At this point, Nadin and his specials were bombarded with brickbats and stones and, upon the orders of Lt-Col L'Estrange – who had just arrived – the crowd was dispersed by the yeomanry and the hussars, many of whom drew their sabres.

The scene was described by Rev. Edward Stanley, Rector of Alderley:

As the cavalry approached the dense mass of people, they used their utmost efforts to escape, but so closely were they pressed in opposite directions by the soldiers, the special constables, the position of the hustings, and their own numbers, that immediate escape was impossible. On their arrival at the hustings, a dreadful confusion ensued. The 15th Hussars then pressed forward, crossing the avenue of constables, which opened to let them through and bent their course towards the Manchester Yeomanry. The people were in a state of utter rout and confusion, leaving the ground strewn with hats and shoes, hundreds were thrown down in the attempt to escape. The cavalry were hurrying in all directions, completing the work of dispersion, which was effected in so short a space of time to appear as if done by magic. During the whole of this confusion, heightened at its close by the rattle of some artillery crossing the square, shrieks were heard in all directions, and as the crowd of people dispersed the effects of the conflict became visible. Some were seen bleeding on the ground and unable to rise, others less severely injured but faint with the loss of blood were retiring slowly or leaning upon the others for support. The whole of this extraordinary scene was the work of a few minutes.

Samuel Bamford, another eyewitness, recounted the scene after the dispersal:

> The field was an open and deserted place. The sun looked down through a sultry and motionless air; the curtains and blinds of the windows were all closed. The hustings remained, with a few broken hewed flag-staves erect, and a torn or gashed banner or two drooping, whilst over the whole field were strewed caps, bonnets, hats, shawls and shoes, and other male and female dress, trampled torn and bloody. The Yeomanry had dismounted; some easing their horses' girths, others adjusting their accoutrements and some were wiping their sabres. Several mounds of human beings still remained where they had fallen, crushed down and smothered; some of them were still groaning, others, with staring eyes were gasping for breath, and others would never breath anymore. All were silent save those low sounds, and the occasional snorting and pawing of steeds.[18]

Michael Bush has recently published the casualty figures from Peterloo, which were obtained from infirmary records. He found there were at least 654 casualties recorded in the register at the Manchester Infirmary. Obviously, there were many other casualties who returned to their homes suffering from non-life-threatening injuries and then went on to nurse themselves without any record being made. The majority of those on the infirmary lists were suffering from sabre wounds and the rest mainly from injuries associated with crushing.[19]

Eleven persons were killed and one was shot and killed later in the day at New Cross. One of those killed was a special constable named John Ashworth, who was crushed somewhere near the hustings. The names of the eleven killed are recorded as:

John Ashton, Cowhill, Chadderton – Sabred
John Ashworth, special constable – Crushed
John Ashworth, Bulls Head Hotel, Manchester – Sabred
Thomas Buckley, Baretrees, Chadderton – Sabred
William Dawson, Saddleworth – Sabred

John Lees, Oldham – Sabred
William Fildes, Kennedy Street, Manchester – Crushed
Arthur O'Niell, Pigeon Street, Manchester – Crushed
Martha Partington, Eccles – Crushed
James Crompton, Barton – Trampled
Mary Heys, Oxford Street, Manchester – Trampled

The actual numbers killed are disputed by historians, some claiming as many as fifteen fatalities.[20] Some of the lists include two Dawsons of Saddleworth, who are more than likely one and the same. Also, the name of John Rhodes of Hopwood is included in some lists, but he died several weeks later from injuries that could not have been linked to Peterloo. Samuel Bamford knew him well and claimed he was a sick man at the time of Peterloo. The coroner agreed and recorded that he had died from natural causes. Sarah Jones is another person listed as having been killed at Peterloo, but no reference is made to the nature of her injuries. Her name appears on only one list and not on any others.

A feature of the casualty lists was that they contained a high number of Irish men and women, either as immigrants or born of Irish parents. According to Professor Bush, ninety-seven casualties were Irish and sixty-seven of these lived in or around New Cross and Great Ancoats Street. These figures suggest that members of the Irish community were strong supporters of the reformist cause, a view supported by Bamford's observation that the Irish came out to support the Middleton contingent as they marched into Manchester en route to St Peter's Field. He wrote that as the Middleton contingent of marchers reached the town, 'they received an ecstatic welcome from the poor Irish weavers at New Cross'.

In an ironic reference to Wellington's famous victory at Waterloo, the tragic event at St Peter's Field was referred to in the press as the Peterloo Massacre. The scene at St Peter's Field that day demonstrates the harsh conditions affecting the people of Manchester at that time. The working people who met there were excluded from parliament, education and the right to combine together to address their grievances at work. Moreover, their impoverishment was exacerbated by the Corn Laws and cyclical unemployment. The magistrates and the political elite, meanwhile, were finding it especially difficult coming to terms with the shock of the French Revolution and the impact of the recently ended French wars, and looked upon Manchester's working class as potential revolutionaries, when previously they were seen as a relatively passive group of workers.

The Hammonds, commenting on the Peterloo Massacre in their book *The Town Labourer*, wrote:

> The revolutions had come together. The French revolution had transformed the minds of the ruling-classes and the industrial revolution had convulsed the world of the working-classes. Politicians like Lord Sidmouth, who saw the poor struggling in the debris of that social upheaval, never imagined that their lot could be made lighter. Discipline, uncompensated by reform and unqualified by concession, was the truest kindness to the working-classes.[21]

After Peterloo, Manchester was in a volatile state, and it fell to Joseph Nadin and his staff to maintain peace and good order as accusations and counter-accusations circulated in every alehouse, public house and factory. Often it was Nadin himself who became the focus of attention as his accusers tried to use his office to score political points against the authorities. *The Times* newspaper reporter, John Tyas, for example, claimed that Nadin had brutally attacked Hunt on the hustings, 'showering repeated blows to his head'.

This accusation by Tyas was repeated in evidence at Hunt's trial, where Hunt himself put the record straight by pointing out that rather than attacking him, it was Nadin who actually rescued him after he had been 'pinned down and struck on the head by soldiers'. Picking up on this point in his summing-up at the end of the trial, the judge commented:

> Hunt has freely confessed that he owed his life upon this occasion to Joseph Nadin. It was Nadin who had come to his assistance and put his hard hat upon his head exclaiming that 'it was a damned shame to treat any man in such a manner'. Hunt was then taken into the house where the magistrates were.[22]

The accuracy of reports published in *The Times* at this time has been challenged by the suggestion of a conspiracy between their reporter, John Tyas, and Archibald Prentice, the editor of the *Manchester Gazette*. In his book *Peterloo: The Case Reopened*, Robert Walmsley argues:

> There seems to have been an agreement reached between the two men on what version of the events each would print. In the Times version of the 16th August, reference is made to 'the Yeomanry actually hacking their way to the hustings'. And yet, five days later, the Times had amended its account to read 'the Yeomanry instantly charged up to the hustings' … The result of

this agreement had been the production of the most misleading, and it is believed, the most far reaching piece of garbled news ever to issue from a newspaper office.[23]

Apart from the tragic consequences which flowed from the actions of those in authority, there were a number of critical issues to emerge from this period. Firstly, at both local and national levels those in government genuinely feared the potential of the working class. Adlington warned Wellington at the time: 'The accounts from Manchester and Leeds are unsatisfactory. A simultaneous explosion appears to be expected.'[24]

Secondly, the idea that the local police were sufficient in numbers and capability to execute the arrest warrant was nothing more than a pipedream. Thirdly, the deployment of the military in support of the civil power was considered a most appropriate response by those in authority, whose common understanding at that time was that the policing of serious public disorder was a job for the military.

Historians such as E.P. Thompson claim that the actions of the military on St Peter's Field were nothing short of 'cold-blooded murder'. He wrote:

> It really was a massacre. The presence of so many women and children was overwhelming testimony to the pacific character of the meeting. The attack was made on this multitude with the venom of panic. It was the panic of class hatred. There is no term for this but class war.[25]

Reid considers the magistrates to have been incompetent and to have panicked under pressure. Walmsley argues that the yeomanry reached the hustings without striking a single blow and that a section of the crowd, determined to knock them off their horses, started to throw stones from the direction of Windmill Street. It was in response to these attacks that the soldiers drew their sabres and cleared the assembled crowd. In support of this view, Walmsley points to the testimony of Mr Roger Entwistle, a local solicitor, who was standing nearby and witnessed this action from an unruly section of the crowd.[26] Apart from Prentice's *Gazette*, nine out of ten newspaper reports relied upon Entwistle's version of events. Along with the factory system and urbanisation, it was felt that after the events of 1819, the cord had been snapped linking the working class from their natural protectors.[27]

Whichever version is considered most reliable, all of the evidence was scrutinised by the High Court in the case of Redford *v*. Birley (1822). Thomas Redford, a journeyman hatter from Audenshaw, Ashton-

under-Lyne, brought an action against Major Hugh Hornby Birley of the
Manchester Yeomanry; Richard Withington, a captain in the same corps;
Alexander Oliver, one of the yeomanry; and Edward Meugher, one of the
yeomanry. The first trial took place at the Spring Assizes, held at Lancaster
Castle on 4 April 1822, when it was alleged by Redford that Major Birley
and others had struck him with their swords, causing cuts and injury. The
jury found in favour of the defendant Birley and the plaintiff went on to
appeal. The case was then listed at the Appeal Court before the most senior
judges in the land.

At the first trial, the defence barrister made the decision not to call the evidence of a number of witnesses, including Joseph Nadin. This was a mistake
he was to put right at the appeal hearing, but not before critics had seized on
the opportunity presented to attack Nadin's conduct at Peterloo.

The Times newspaper reporter John Tyas mischievously reported that the
judge had stated: 'There is no evidence of Nadin's inability to execute the
warrant as he has claimed all along.' To the reader this statement appears to
be a criticism of Nadin made by the trial judge. What the newspaper report
failed to mention, however, was that the judge's comment was a reference to
the failure on the part of the prosecution barrister to call Nadin as a witness.
According to the trial papers, the exact words used by the judge were:

> What Nadin's reason was, and whether that was the reason upon which we
> should be warranted in asking, we are left considerably at a loss, because we
> have not the testimony of Nadin in that respect. If Nadin knew facts which
> satisfied him that he could not execute the warrant at that place, Nadin
> should have been put in the box as a witness in order to have shown that
> fact to you.[28]

At the Appeal Court hearing in London, Nadin entered the witness box and
gave his evidence on oath. He told the court that he had recently retired
from the office of Deputy Constable but was still active as a special constable. He went on to tell the court that he had between 300 and 400 special
constables assembled in a double line in St Peter's Field on the morning of
16 August 1819:[29]

> Mr Justice Cross: 'From all that you had observed that morning amongst the
> multitude previous to your receiving the warrant did you deem it practi-
> cable to execute the warrant without military aid?'

Nadin: 'I did not.'

Mr Cross: 'Did you think it could be attempted with safety to the lines of the peace officers without that assistance?'

Nadin: 'I durst not do it, from the reception I had received a few days before.'

Mr Cross: 'On what occasion?'

Nadin: 'The execution of a warrant on a former occasion days before. The boroughreeve and constables and me and two or three beadles were called to New Cross; the paper sticker was posting bills. We went to the place where it was said our men were in the house, we went through the mob. When we got through the mob, there was a shower of stones came upon us.'

Mr Cross: 'What became of the peace officers?'

Nadin: 'Mr. Moore and Mr. Clayton got away and Andrew and me and two beadles could not get away well; we got on the outside and turned down Oldham Street and then Mr. Moore and Mr. Clayton were bringing in the military.'

Mr Cross: 'Then the recollections of the transaction and what you saw on the 14th August contributed to deter you from executing the warrant without military aid?'

Nadin: 'Yes. I had a warrant to arrest Mr. Hunt but it could not be attempted without the assistance of the military. I advised Mr. Hulton that it would be out of our power without the aid of the military. The crowd in the field had linked arms. I asked the specials to withdraw to the magistrate's house to let the Yeomanry come down. I followed the military down.'

Mr Cross: 'Did you see them cutting the people at right and left, as they went along with their swords?'

Nadin: 'No, I did not. I was the man first at the hustings and I pulled Johnson off I believe Andrew took him from me.'

At the end of the hearing, the ruling went as follows:

Mr Justice Bailey: 'I am of the opinion that in this case no evidence which ought to have been received was rejected; that no evidence was admitted which ought not to have been admitted. There is abundance of evidence in this case and I say in this case, for the first time, that without the aid of the military, the warrant could not have been executed.'

Mr Justice Best: 'All they [the yeomanry] had to do in the first instance, was to advance and take the persons on the hustings into custody; but if they were resisted, that resistance rendered it necessary that they should do all the acts made the subject of the complaint against them. They were acting under the authority of the magistrates. We have been told that the conduct of these magistrates was scandalous, and that they might have dispersed the meeting without the military. That is an assertion contradicted by all the evidence and by common sense.'

Lord Chief Justice Holroyd: 'If the magistrates had suffered them to act as they please instead of putting an end to the meeting, no man could say that the town of Manchester would have been safer for that night. It appears to me that the magistrates acted lawfully, justifiably and with promptitude that entitled them to the gratitude of the neighbourhood and the thanks of the country.

The military acted in aid of the civil power, because Nadin says it was inadequate for the purpose and there are many persons who support this. There is no excuse for saying that this was a mere pretence for letting loose the military and draw back the civil power.'[30]

At the conclusion of the case, the Appeal Court turned down Redford's appeal and supported the decisions made by Nadin and the magistrates. The radicals' version of events was also overturned, although their staunch advocate Archibald Prentice refused to accept it, and continued with the opinion that it was a deliberately orchestrated 'massacre'.

The defendant in the case, Major Hugh Hornby Birley, came from one of Manchester's most prominent Conservative families, who owned cotton mills in Chorlton-on-Medlock. He went on to become the first president of Manchester's Chamber of Commerce.

William Cobbett, who was in America at the time of Peterloo, continued to incur the wrath of Lord Liverpool's government, especially that of the Home

Secretary Lord Sidmouth. He joined the ranks of those parliamentary reformers led by Major John Cartwright, who campaigned for an end to existing corruptions and the introduction of parliamentary constituencies based on population and the extension of the franchise. In the eyes of Lord Liverpool, such views were not only dangerous but 'smacked of Jacobism'. Following the Reform Act of 1832, Cobbett was elected as MP for Oldham.

Lord Liverpool's response to Peterloo, and the continuing political agitation for parliamentary reform, was to introduce legislation in support of local office-holders, which became known as the Six Acts of Parliament. They were as follows:

1. To prohibit any gatherings for arming or drilling;
2. To give magistrates 'in the disturbed areas' powers to search for arms;
3. To prevent defendants from securing delays by postponing their answers to specific charges;
4. To prohibit meetings of more than 50 persons without magistrates' consent;
5. To indemnify magistrates against the consequences of casualties suffered in dispersing illegal assemblies;
6. To increase the penalties for writing seditious libels.[31]

The parliamentary reform movement did not go away after Peterloo. As we shall see in the next chapter, it was to find expression in the emerging Chartist movement, which to a great extent represented the climax of working-class struggle for parliamentary representation.

Notes

1. J. Kay, *The Moral and Physical Condition of the Working Classes*, 1832, p.294.
2. E.P. Thompson, *The Making of the English Working Class*, 1963, p.553.
3. M. Thomis and P. Holt, *Threats of Revolution in Britain 1789–1848*, 1977, p.33.
4. R. Reid, *The Peterloo Massacre*, 1989, p.25.
5. D. Bythell, *The Handloom Weavers*, 1969, p.30.
6. J.D. Marshall, *Lancashire*, 1974, p.64.
7. C. Aspin, *Lancashire: The First Industrial Society*, 1969, p.44.
8. E. Baines, *Lancashire*, Vol.2, 1824, p.122.
9. A. Prentice, *Historical Sketches and Personal Recollections*, 1851, p.30.
10. S. Bamford, *Passages in the Life of a Radical*, 1839.
11. S. Bamford, *Passages in the Life of a Radical*, 1839.
12. J. Marlow, *The Peterloo Massacre*, 1969, p.34.
13. S. Bamford, *Passages in the Life of a Radical*, 1839, p.13.

14. *Manchester Gazette*, 7 August 1819.
15. Robert Reid, *The Peterloo Massacre*, 1989, p.145.
16. R. Walmsley, *Peterloo: The Case Reopened*, 1969.
17. See HO papers 42.18.
18. S. Bamford, *Passages in the Life of a Radical*, 1839.
19. M. Bush, *The Casualties of Peterloo*, 2005, pp.28–9.
20. J. Marlow, *The Peterloo Massacre*, 1969.
21. J. and B. Hammond, *The Town Labourer, 1760–1832*, 1917, p.94.
22. *Manchester Observer*, 29 May 1820.
23. R. Walmsley, *Peterloo: The Case Reopened*, 1969, p.508.
24. J. Black, *The Hanoverians*, 2004, p.157.
25. E.P. Thompson, *The Making of the English Working Class*, 1963, p.685.
26. R. Walmsley, *Peterloo: The Case Reopened*, 1969, p.146.
27. F. Engels, *The Condition of the Working Class in England*, 1892, p.685.
28. State Trials, Sessional Parliamentary Papers 458–60.
29. R. Walmsley, *Peterloo: The Case Reopened*, 1969, p.166.
30. Peterloo Trial Notes 4–9 April 1922.
31. E.J. Evans, *Britain Before the Reform Act of 1832*, 1989, p.24.

4

CHARTISM, ANTI-CORN LAW LEAGUE AND THE BIRTH OF THE LABOUR PARTY

At first, the working class in Manchester were not politically radical. At the beginning of the nineteenth century they were more likely to be described as supporters of Church and King. This loyalty to the state and its institutions had been reinforced by feelings of nationalism brought about by their involvement in the Napoleonic Wars and the threat of a French invasion, but it was soon to be challenged by the state's repressive responses to their frustrated appeals, to the monarch's distant silence, and to the Church's association with the agricultural Corn Laws.

By 1830, the question of parliamentary reform was placed high on the political agenda, and, in the months that followed, several motions were presented in the House of Commons calling for the abolition of rotten boroughs and a redistribution of seats in favour of the growing manufacturing towns like Manchester. Cornwall, for example, returned forty-four members, whereas London returned ten and Manchester none.

Pressure for reform was delayed for a further twelve months due to two extraneous events. In June 1831, King George IV died, and then, in September, tragedy struck at the opening of the Manchester–Liverpool railway, which saw William Huskisson MP run over by a carriage on the tracks after he had left his carriage during a temporary stop.

The general election held in August, a consequence of the death of the king, returned a large number of MPs to the House of Commons, who had come to recognise that the mood in the country demanding reform of parliament had reached fever pitch. For example, Henry Broughton, MP for

Leeds, Sheffield and Huddersfield, pledged that reform must become a top
priority if good order was to be maintained. Charles Lamb, MP for Enfield,
declared: 'Poor Enfield that has been peaceful hitherto has caught the inflam-
matory fever.' Many other members went on to lend their support to Lord
Russell's Great Reform Bill as it progressed through the house.' The Act was
a tremendous first step as it extended the franchise and redistributed seats,
with Manchester gaining two seats in the process, but for the vast majority of
non-property-owning inhabitants, the reality was that the provisions in the
Bill made no difference at all.

Mark Phillips and Charles Poulett Thomson became Manchester's first
elected MPs, with the support of the majority of 'bosses' and enfranchised
property owners in the new constituency. Mark Phillips was the eldest son
of Robert Phillips of the Park, Manchester, and Charles Thomson was a
member of a Whig family who traded in cotton and other goods, with offices
in London and St Petersburg. His outspoken views on free trade and parliamentary reform no doubt made him an attractive candidate for local Liberals.

The new parliamentary borough comprised of Manchester, Ardwick,
Beswick, Bradford, Cheetham Hill, Chorlton-on-Medlock, Harpurhey,
Hulme and Newton. Not surprisingly, the town of Manchester dominated
the constituency, with 142,000 out of 187,000 living within its boundaries.

In reality, the Reform Act itself was a watered-down version of the one
that William Cobbett and friends had fought for, but at least industrial towns
like Manchester had been enfranchised and it was hoped that the returning
MPs would force parliament to adopt a more reformist second Bill. Its significance in opening the door, ever so slightly, ought not to be underestimated.

Having failed to secure political rights for working men, many working-
class activists from all parts of the country adopted the aims of the 'people's
charter'. The charter was published in 1838 and had six main aims: universal
manhood suffrage; the payment of MPs; abolition of the property qualification for voting; the holding of secret ballots; annual parliaments; and equal
electoral districts. The campaigns to secure these rights were prominent for
over a decade, up to 1848, when the Chartist movement suffered an anti-
climax from which it never recovered.

Chartism found its main roots within industrial communities in South
Lancashire, the West Riding of Yorkshire, South Wales, Leicester, Coventry,
Birmingham and the East End of London. It was well supported in the
Manchester area, particularly in Oldham, Bolton, Ashton-under-Lyne and
Rochdale, and especially in those districts which had a large number of
domestic handloom weavers, whose plight had become especially acute at

this time. George Smith, the manager of a Manchester textile firm employing 1,000 domestic weavers across Lancashire, reported: 'Out of 32 handloom calico manufacturers whom I know personally, 28 have failed and more than half of all persons who have engaged in that trade in Manchester who have not added spinning to their business have also failed.'[2]

One of the main characteristics of the Chartist movement was a common culture in which political education was spread among working men and women at lectures, meetings and open-air rallies. At these venues, Chartists shared a secular fellowship, a common purpose and a commitment to the politicisation of the working class. This culture was reinforced through the circulation of the movement's own newspaper, the *Northern Star*.

The *Northern Star* was founded by Feargus O'Connor in 1833, and its Manchester branch was headed by O'Connor's agent Abel Heywood. It was reported that the *Star* was so popular that a special coach had to be hired to transport copies from town to town in the Manchester area.

From the very beginning, however, the Chartist movement had a serious flaw in its make-up. It lacked a leader who could unite its two main factions. On the one hand, men like O'Connor, originally of Irish gentry stock and who had trained to become a barrister, made great use of fiery language in calling upon working-class resistance and use of force against their oppressors. 'Force would have to be used to obtain justice and the acknowledgement of right,' he proclaimed.

Another fiery orator, whose language often put him at loggerheads with fellow Chartists and the authorities, was Rev. Joseph Rayner Stephens, who was particularly active in the Manchester area and in the West Riding. An ex-Wesleyan minister, Stephens' headquarters were in Ashton-under-Lyne. At a meeting held at Oldham on 8 November 1838 he advocated that since the workers had had their share of misery, it was time for the other half to have theirs 'by us burning mills, blowing out their brains and pulling down the Bastilles'.[3]

Manchester-born mill worker James Leach was another Chartist activist and writer who identified an inherent conflict between the middle class and the working class. He wrote: 'The executive of the modern state is but a committee for managing the common affairs of the bourgeoisie.' Many of his writings were to find their way into Marx and Engels' *The Communist Manifesto*, which is not all that surprising as Leach and Engels were to become close friends in the 1840s.[4]

In the Manchester area, 'physical force' Chartist supporters were exclusively working class, with textile workers being the largest group. They were followed by coal miners, blacksmiths, silversmiths, mechanical engineers,

joiners, bricklayers, plasterers, painters and small shopkeepers. Among the
most prominent speakers and agitators were tradesmen such as Elizah Dixon,
watchmaker and Peterloo veteran; Christopher Dean, stonemason; William
Aitken, cotton spinner; James Snowball, joiner; and James Leach, mill worker.
Each of them had been arrested and served terms of imprisonment.

In contrast to the 'physical force' Chartists, the 'moral' or 'peaceful' wing
was led by men such as William Lovett, a London shopkeeper, who argued
that the real strength of the working class lay not in violent conflict but in
self-improvement through education, Sunday schools and temperance, all of
which were subsumed under the ideal of 'respectability'.

Undoubtedly, the Chartists caused the ruling class serious cause for concern, especially when some of O'Connor's supporters threatened to bring
down the government if their demands contained in the charter were not
met. Against the background of revolutions taking place across Europe in the
year 1848, the news that the Chartists were planning a National Convention
in London in April that year prompted the government to arrange for Queen
Victoria and her family to be spirited away to Osborne House on the Isle of
Wight until such time as the police and military had subdued the gathering
and restored peace to the capital.

At 9 a.m. on 10 April 1848, the convention's supporters assembled in John
Street and marched down Tottenham Court Road, via Holborn, to Farrington
Street, crossed Blackfriars Bridge, and reached Kennington Common by
11.30 a.m., where some 3,000 had gathered. Another contingent started out
at Stepney Green in the East End and arrived on the Common with 2,000
supporters. The largest group was in Russell Square and proceeded down
Walworth Road to the Common with 10,000 supporters. The organisers had
expected hundreds of thousands, but in the event not more than an estimated
20,000 turned out.

Whilst the numbers in attendance proved disappointing, the authorities
were leaving nothing to chance and deployed around 8,000 soldiers on the
streets, with 4,000 policemen put on alert, and another 8,000 special constables enrolled for duty.[5]

The Chartists were never going to generate enough support to overthrow
the state and begin a revolution. They failed essentially on two counts. First,
the reformed police proved much too strong and well organised; and second,
not only were they divided, but by 1848 their membership had fallen off from
what it had been a decade before.

As Kidd's research shows, region to region support and membership were
in decline. Out of 1,009 areas generally supportive of Chartism, only 209

had active Chartist organisations in 1848. Moreover, the economic conditions that had driven so many into supporting the movement had, ever so slightly, started to improve, and this prompted membership and support to decline.[6]

The upturn in the trade cycle by mid-century saw a retreat from the politics of despair and a lowering of the political temperature. In essence, the critical issues that led to working-class participation in political movements such as Chartism were resolved (at least in part) by improved employment opportunities and wages. Moreover, working conditions in the factories had improved with the introduction of the Ten Hours Act, which restricted the hours worked by women and children. Rev. Stephens recognised the impact of economic improvements on the movement's decline when he wrote: 'Chartism thrived most when people were hungry and unemployed.'[7]

In addition, the government demonstrated, through its deployment of large numbers of police and military, its determination and capability to put down any signs of disaffection or revolt by force if necessary. This kind of repressive action was only to be expected from a government presiding over such a 'ruthless, competitive society', according to A.N. Wilson. 'This was a male dominated society, stamping on its victims and discarding its weaker members with all the devastating relentlessness of mutant species in Darwin's vision of nature itself.'[8]

The government's message was reinforced by Sir Charles Napier, recently appointed commander of the army in the North West, who conducted a tour of 'the most disaffected areas around Manchester', after which he summoned the leaders of the Chartists to a meeting and warned them that he would be prepared to 'match them with cannon and musket at the first signs of unrest and violence'.[9]

To a great extent, the Chartist movement was exclusively working class. Whilst there may have been a small number of middle-class radicals who supported the idea of manhood suffrage, they never made a common cause with them. This separation arose out of the fear generated by the members of the 'physical force' wing, who were perceived as totally lacking respect for property or authority.

The Chartist movement did not disappear overnight, however. Many old Chartists were assimilated into the two main political parties, while others became members of the co-operative movement, which was starting up in Manchester, Rochdale and Oldham. The famous Rochdale Pioneers opened their shop in Toad Lane, Rochdale, on 21 December 1844, with several Chartists featured among its twenty-eight original members.

Some old Chartists were to join embryonic trade unions after the lifting of the prohibitive Combination Acts in 1871. Unions such as the Cotton

Spinners, Engineers and Coal Miners all had old Chartists among their members, although they were not warmly welcomed by employers, who came to view them with deep suspicion.[10]

John Walton points out that in 1853 there were just fifty-eight provincial branches of the movement remaining, of which ten were in south-east Lancashire, located at Manchester, Rochdale, Oldham and Ashton-under-Lyne. In the following year, an estimated 2,000 supporters and their families attended a rally on Blackstone Edge, north of Rochdale, but this was the last time a large crowd gathered in the name of Chartism.[11]

The more settled economic climate helped to improve relations between masters and workers. The president of the Cotton Spinners Union reported: 'There is a spirit of cordiality in the factory.' The secretary of the National Association of United Trades endorsed this view when he wrote: 'A good feeling has arisen between the employer and the employed.' That these once-hostile parties came together to form an alliance in opposition to the dreaded Corn Laws is, in some respects, testimony to this changing mood, albeit the two sides were approaching the problem from different standpoints – the price of bread and opposition to protectionism.

On 24 September 1838, 30,000 people gathered at a public meeting on Kersal Moor, on the outskirts of Manchester, to begin a movement aimed at repealing the Corn Laws, the success of which contrasted sharply to the decline of the Chartists. The founding of the Anti-Corn Law Association set in motion a series of events that was to lead to a triumph of the industrial over the agricultural interests, and the adoption of a policy of free trade over protectionism by the government.[12]

The strength of support for the League (it soon changed its title from an association) varied from place to place. It was very strong in Manchester and its satellite towns, whereas in the non-cotton towns of Liverpool and St Helens, for example, it attracted little support. It was also blessed in having two effective and united leaders in Richard Cobden and John Bright, the latter becoming more active in the movement after his wife died in 1841.

An unintended consequence of the League's activities was that it managed to drive a wedge between the Christian churches. Members of the Nonconformist churches were strong supporters and viewed the Corn Laws as being associated with the established Church by way of its rural gentry links. The Church of England came to be seen by many in the manufacturing towns as having profited from keeping the price of bread artificially high. Richard Cobden wrote in 1842:

The church clergy are almost to a man guilty of causing the present distress by upholding the Corn Laws – they themselves having an interest in the high price of bread. We have, I believe, the majority of every religious denomination with us. We have them almost en-masse, both ministers and lay men; and I believe the only body against us, as a body, are the members of the Church of England.[13]

Eventually, after seven years of agitation, the dreaded Corn Laws were repealed on 26 July 1846. Repeal was achieved principally due to the conversion of Peel, Russell and others in the Tory party to the principles of free trade and the perils of protectionism. Whereas Chartism had been overwhelmingly a working-class movement, the Anti-Corn Law League was overwhelmingly middle class, with only limited working-class support. Richard Cobden confirmed this when he wrote in 1841: 'I don't deny that the working classes generally have attended our lectures and signed our petitions; but I will admit that so far as the fervour and efficiency of our agitation has gone, it has eminently been a middle class agitation.'[14] Few would deny, however, that both classes benefited from the repeal of the Corn Laws.

The significance of their achievement was not lost on the great temperance campaigner Joseph Livesey, who wrote: 'Comparing the last twenty years with the previous thirty years, I don't hesitate to say that free trade saved this country from revolution and has been the forerunner to that contentment, tranquillity and progress which have marked this latter period.'[15]

Whereas the Corn Laws were a symbol of the political controls exercised by the landowning, agricultural interest, their repeal signified the growing strength and influence of the reforming middle class in manufacturing towns like Manchester. Hereafter, however, Manchester's middle class returned to a more conservative, self-satisfied outlook, and went on to elect the city's first Conservative MP in 1868.[16]

Richard Cobden went on to become the MP for Stockport, and John Bright became MP for Manchester after a brief spell as MP for Durham.

The reported 'spirit of cordiality' was to be seriously put to the test in 1862 when Manchester and other towns in south-east Lancashire were hit and hit hard by the effects of the cotton famine, which had followed on from the American Civil War. What was to prove especially significant was the quiet response to temporary mill closures and the severe hardship felt by textile families and those workers in associated trades. Where protest did exist, it was in isolated pockets in just a few areas, notably in Ashton-under-Lyne and Stalybridge, with hardly any recorded in the boundaries of Manchester.[17] The reasons for this relatively quiet response are closely related to the long-term transition from street protest to responsible trade unionism on the one hand, and to the workers' identification with and support for the anti-slavery movement, which had given the American Civil War conflict a moral dimension.

On 31 December 1862, a meeting of textile workers was held in the Free Trade Hall, which resolved to support the Unionists in their fight against slavery and to write a letter to President Lincoln supporting his stand. Many speakers compared the plight of the textile workers to that of the plantation slaves, highlighting long hours in the factories, unhealthy conditions in terraced houses owned by the bosses, and inflated prices paid for adulterated food at corner shops, which were also owned by the bosses. It was claimed that exploitation in the production of cotton was what united the factory worker in Manchester with the plantation worker in the Southern States of America.

On 19 January 1863, the President replied, saying that he was 'deeply moved by the sufferings which the working people of Manchester are called to endure in this crisis'. This exchange was to lead to the erection of a commemorative statue of President Lincoln in Brazennose Street, off Albert Square in the city centre.[18]

In this period of acute hardship, members of the working class and their trade unions showed themselves to be responsible and conciliatory in industrial affairs, so much so that both the authorities and the employers no longer feared them as being a threat to property or to the state. To a great extent this demonstrable change in attitude and behaviour persuaded the political class that the working class had shown themselves well fitted for 'admission to the constitution' and, as a consequence, household suffrage was extended under the Reform Acts of 1867 and 1884. In 1871, workers' representation through trade unions became legally recognised.

Although times were hard in the 1860s, members of Manchester's working class remained resolute and determined to engage in self-improvement activities to raise themselves out of poverty and ignorance. For example, in June 1862, a meeting of unemployed workers held in Stevenson Square passed a resolution opposing what they considered to be the 'demeaning labour test' of the Poor Law Guardians. In its place they proposed a 'school test' or 'learning test', whereby recipients of relief would attend adult schools to learn basic literacy and crafts such as carpentry or sewing. The resolution was accepted by the Manchester Board of Guardians and soon took off across all of Lancashire, where empty mills were converted into schoolrooms and teachers recruited on a voluntary basis. One of the converted buildings in

Manchester was located in City Road, Hulme, and became known as the Institute for the Unemployed.[19]

Whilst it may be claimed that some workers withdrew their savings from credit clubs and building societies to offset some of the worst excesses of the cotton famine, such action applied to only a small percentage of workers and, as Walton points out, 'Savings did not prevent destitution, they merely delayed it, although the habits and mindset of saving may well have been conducive to the silent endurance of adversity. Secondly, the cotton famine was less likely to generate widespread hostility because its causes were perceived to be external and short term.'[20]

The virtue of self-help among the working class was promoted by Samuel Smiles in his best-selling book of the same title. Smiles preached the virtues of hard work, thrift and the capacity of the working man to advance himself and his family through sobriety. He was the editor of the *Leeds Times* and a strong supporter of William Cobbett and the Anti-Corn Law League.

To a great extent, self-help initiatives helped to anchor the working class and their associations to the established social and political order. The discipline and obedience that underpinned them was reinforced through an expansion in church-building right across Manchester, as the churches tried to catch up with the rapid rise in population. According to Leatherbarrow, Manchester's Bishop Prince Lee consecrated 110 new churches between 1848 and 1869, while twenty existing churches were refurnished or rebuilt. Between the years 1870 and 1885, his successor, Bishop Fraser, consecrated another 105 churches. Anglican church-building was in step with Nonconformist and Catholic expansion, motivated by competition, a genuine desire to 'civilise' the masses, and a sincere hope to save souls.[21] The overall impact no doubt proved a distraction from the pursuit of radical political remedies for secular problems.

By the 1890s, the idea that the working class required a separate political party that would promote the ideology of wealth redistribution, as embodied in socialism, was very much under discussion following a breakdown in the good working relations which had characterised the 1860s era. A major strike called by the Cotton Spinners Union closed down many factories in Lancashire in 1892, and lasted for five months. The following year, mill owners ordered a 10 per cent cut in wage rates across the textile industry to offset a slump in trade. The workers' trade unions refused to accept the cut and the owners' associations ordered an immediate lock-out. As a consequence, factories across Manchester and in most parts of Lancashire shut down completely, intending to drive the workforce to agree to a settlement. The trade unions stuck it out for twenty weeks before agreeing to a 3 per cent wage cut. The years of conciliation and collaboration between factory owners and workers had now evaporated to be replaced by mistrust and in many cases open conflict.

The idea of labour representation in parliament was given a further boost in 1894 when the Liberal government imposed a duty on the importation into India of cotton yarns and cloth, despite a promise made to the cotton unions not to do so. Textile trade unions pointed out the futility of applying political pressure on supposedly sympathetic MPs who reneged on their promises.

Notwithstanding these setbacks, the Cotton Spinners Union remained hostile to the ideas associated with socialism, in part because of their historical sense of superiority, seeing themselves as occupying a position at the top of the cotton industry hierarchy. From their viewpoint, socialists were those disruptive elements who made periodic attempts to organise the piecers independently of the spinners. And, as the piecers were positioned at the bottom of the cotton hierarchy, so the ideas of socialism were seen as being associated with the inferior section of workers.

A tipping point was reached in 1899, when 129 trade union delegates assembled at their conference in London, to be joined by recently formed socialist organisations, including the Fabian Society, Social Democratic Federation and the Independent Labour Party. At the meeting, a resolution was passed that they form a Labour Representative Committee to explore the possibility of forming a Labour Party to represent all workers in parliament. Included on that historic committee were Keir Hardie, Ramsay MacDonald and George Bernard Shaw.

The formation of the Labour Representative Committee was testimony to the disappointment Liberalism had been to its working-class supporters, especially the textile workers. The loss of Gladstone as leader was felt particularly badly, with a succession of leaders from Rosebery and Harcourt to Campbell-Bannerman failing to measure up. Moreover, the enfranchisement of the working class had by now moved labour representation to the top of the working-class political agenda.

In many respects, despite Keir Hardie's rallying call that all sections of the labour movement must unite under one banner, the founding fathers were bedevilled by disunity. For example, socialist groups like the Marxist SDF sought to make the new party an instrument of 'class war', but their resolution to that effect was soundly defeated by a large majority.

The ILP was a more numerously supported body. Formed in Manchester in 1893, one of its leaders was Robert Blatchford, editor of the *Clarion* newspaper, who advocated temperance, healthy pursuits and respectability, as being 'the most genuine aims for a working class party'. The socialism of the ILP 'meant many things to many people' but it became clear that it was averse to ideas of 'class struggle' and 'revolutionary politics'.[22]

At the 1900 general election, the embryonic Labour Party put forward fifteen candidates but only two were elected – Keir Hardie at Merthyr and Richard Bell at Derby. The breakthrough came in 1906 when twenty-nine of the fifty-one candidates were successful, all of them with explicit trade union backing. At Manchester, Labour won two out of the six seats, returning John Robert Clynes and George Davy Kelley as their elected representatives in parliament. John Robert Clynes had been a founder member of the ILP and took the Miles Platting seat from the Liberals. He successfully held the seat for the next thirty-nine years, apart from a brief period between 1930 and 1935.

John Robert Clynes was born in Oldham on 27 March 1869, of illiterate Irish-born parents, Patrick and Bridget, who had a family of seven children. He left elementary school at the age of 10 to work part time as a 'little piecer' at the Dowry mill in Turner Street, Lees. He started work at 6 a.m. and after lunch went to the local school until 4 p.m. At the age of 12, he worked in the mill as a full-time piecer. He became an active trade unionist and was elected president of the Oldham Trades and Labour Council at the tender age of 21. He claimed that he was an avid reader and had learned to read and write at the local Co-operative store's reading rooms. Clynes opposed militant class politics, always preferring negotiation and persuasion. He argued:

> To set ourselves to organise the workers of Britain on a Marxist, Russian or French plan would be setting ourselves a task inappropriate to our conditions and fatal for our purpose. We offer something quite different from the two main parties. We went out with a spiritual appeal, as well as to win material concessions.[23]

He went on to become deputy leader of the House of Commons in 1924 and then Home Secretary in Ramsay MacDonald's government of 1929. He retired as MP for Miles Platting in 1945 to look after his disabled wife Mary at their home in London.

Parliamentary politics had now replaced street protest and pressure-group activity for the working class in Manchester. It was evolutionary rather than being revolutionary, although for a time there were many who were fearful that Manchester might lead the country into some kind of violent upheaval, along lines similar to what had been witnessed in France at the end of the eighteenth century, and repeated in 1830 and 1848.

Notes

1. E. Pearce, *Reform!: The Fight for the 1832 Reform Act*, 2004, p.58.
2. D. Bythell, *The Handloom Weavers*, 1969.
3. D. Fisher, *The Oldham Chronicle*, 1 July 1972.
4. F. Engels, *The Condition of the Working Class in England*, 1892, p.242 (English edition).
5. A. Kidd, *Manchester*, 1993, pp.63–7.
6. K.T. Hoppen, *The Mid-Victorian Generation*, 2000, p.130.
7. A. Briggs, *Chartist Studies*, 1962, pp.372–405.
8. A.N. Wilson, *The Victorians*, 2002, p.120.
9. A. Briggs, *Chartist Studies*, 1962, pp.372–405.
10. F.C. Mather, *Public Order in the Age of the Chartists*, 1959.
11. J.K. Walton, *Lancashire*, 1987.
12. C. Aspin, *Lancashire: The First Industrial Society*, 1969, p.138.
13. H. Perkin, *The Origins of Modern English Society*, 1969, p.350.
14. Ibid., p.315.
15. J. Livesey, *The Moral Reformer*, 1868, p.125.
16. H. Perkin, *The Origins of Modern English Society*, 1969, p.371.
17. J. Foster, *Class Struggle in the 19th Century*, 1974, pp.232–8.
18. N. Longmate, *The Hungry Mills*, 1978, p.174.
19. J.K. Walton, *Lancashire*, 1987.
20. J.K. Walton, *Lancashire*, 1987.
21. J. Leatherbarrow, *The Victorian Period Piece*, 1954.
22. J. Cronin, *New Labour's Past*, 2004, p.24.
23. J.R. Clynes, *Memoirs*, 1957, p.103.

1 A Manchester watchman on duty. (Courtesy of Greater Manchester Police)

2 Joseph Nadin, Deputy Constable of Manchester, 1802–20. (Courtesy of the John Rylands Library, Manchester University)

3 Samuel Bamford, Middleton radical poet.

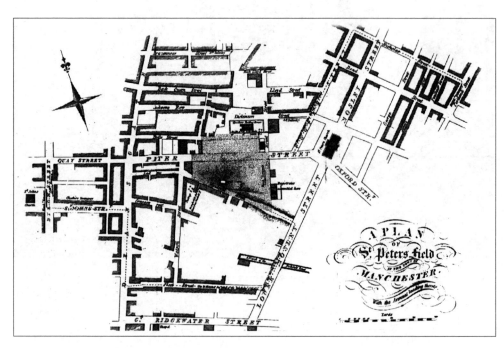

4 Plan of St Peter's Field, site of the Peterloo Massacre.

5 Manchester police on parade, 1844. (Courtesy of Greater Manchester Police)

6 Police prison van attacked by Fenians, 1867.

7 Police Sergeant Charles Brett, shot and killed by Fenians, 1867. (Courtesy of Greater Manchester Police)

8 Charlie Peace, notorious burglar and murderer.

9 Captain William Henry Palin, Chief Constable of Manchester, 1858–79. (Courtesy of Greater Manchester Police)

10 Jerome Caminada,
Detective Chief Inspector.
(Courtesy of Greater
Manchester Police)

11 John Robert Clynes,
MP for Miles Platting.
(Courtesy of National
Portrait Gallery)

12 Sir Robert Peacock, Chief Constable of Manchester, 1898–1926. (Courtesy of Greater Manchester Police)

5

CRIME AND CRIMINALS

It is in the nature of this study that a topic such as crime is examined over a period of time, so as to identify the extent of change and to highlight some of the various issues raised, such as the unreliability of official crime statistics and the accuracy of contemporaries' perceptions of crime and its different causes. In the process, we shall be taking a look at some of the characters whose criminal exploits made them notorious and infamous beyond the boundaries of Manchester.

Crime is a subject that does not exist in abstraction but is influenced by many processes taking place in the wider environment. According to McCabe, 'Crime is a complex interaction between different processes, from the state having defined certain behaviours as criminal, to state agencies – like the police – who may or may not process those responsible and then the courts, who may or may not punish those prosecuted and found guilty'.[1]

All of these processes and more take place against a cultural backcloth or context, which is constantly changing in response to events, the pace of which, in the nineteenth century, was justifiably described as 'revolutionary'.

In providing a definition of the word 'crime', McCabe goes on to explain that it is laden with pitfalls: 'There is no word in the whole lexicon of legal and criminological terms which is so elusive of precise definition as the word crime.' This statement is well illustrated by Angus Bethune Reach's comment in 1849, when he reported in the *News Chronicle*:

In Manchester, where standpipes and public taps are erected, the charge by
the water company is about ten shillings a year for every household, the
inmates of which use the convenience. Of all the petty thefts which occur
in Manchester however, none – although they do not appear in the official
police returns – are so common as theft from water taps and pumps.[2]

In the eighteenth and early nineteenth centuries, criminal justice was essentially a local issue, with the Court Leet and County Justices of the Peace
having responsibility for law and order in Manchester. It was not until the
second half of the nineteenth century that the state assumed control of most
of the functions of the judicial system, whether that be the financing and
inspecting of the reformed police, or the appointment and financing of magistrates' petty-sessional courts. State support for the police was also provided
by the military, whose deployment in the event of outbreaks of serious disorder continued until after the mid-century period.

Any understanding of crime and criminals in this early period relies on
contemporary accounts in support of official statistics, which themselves are
unreliable measures of what was actually taking place. Although the present
complete series of judicial statistics only commenced in 1856–57, there were
earlier, somewhat crude, attempts at recording criminal behaviours stretch-
ing back to 1810. These statistical returns are to be found in the House of
Commons Select Committee reports, as well as books, pamphlets and jour-
nals supplied by contemporaries, including Patrick Colquhoun, a magistrate,
and Henry Mayhew, journalist.

Patrick Colquhoun's habit of providing various Commissions of Inquiry
with his personal estimates of crime was openly challenged before the Select
Committee on Police in 1816:

> The great foible of Dr. Colquhoun, who excites distrust in all his statements,
> is the assumption of accurate calculation upon subjects that do not admit to
> any calculation at all. He can have no possible data on which to found the
> conclusions to which he has come, as to the number of houses open for the
> reception of stolen goods.[3]

Apprehensions made by the police might be viewed as an indicator both
of criminality and of the efficiency of the police. However, in the Chief
Constable's reports for the years 1845–47, there was a marked reduction in
apprehensions, which had more to do with changes in policy introduced by
the Chief Constable. Chief Constable Willis reported:

In circumstances where an offence of a trivial nature has been committed then it is deemed expedient to take the offender's name and address and summon him before the courts rather than take him into custody. By adopting this conciliatory course of action many unnecessary apprehensions are avoided, order has been re-established and maintained, and a better and more kindly feeling has been induced, without any compromise of duty between the inhabitants and the police force.

People living in Manchester knew all too well from their life experiences that most crimes went unrecorded and undetected for all manner of reasons, not least that it was pointless involving the police, who were seen by most people as being at best inefficient and at worst useless. This placed greater reliance on court statistics, but it was also known that changes in the law or in the practices of different courts often made any meaningful comparison unreliable. For example, some judges relied on their discretionary powers when sentencing juvenile offenders for criminal offences, which were often quite different from those offences listed on the indictment, in order to speed up the judicial process or set a more appropriate tariff.[4]

By the same process, crimes such as burglary, which had been tried before the Assize Courts up to 1835, were being reduced to larceny so that they could be tried before the Quarter Sessions (a lower court), thereby reducing the delay between committal and trial for the benefit of the criminal, who was being held in custody for long periods awaiting a trial date.[5]

This somewhat benevolent or sympathetic side to judicial discretion was not always at the forefront of sentencing, however. Take the case of a young girl, Ann Wild, who had the misfortune to appear before the Manchester magistrates in 1836. She had been found by the police wandering the streets of the town centre at a late hour and was taken to the police station at Newton Street for her own safety. As she waited in this 'place of safety', Ann Wild was charged with an offence under the Vagrancy Act of 1824, despite the fact that she lived close by in Back Piccadilly and her father was in employment as a shoemaker. It was reported that she had a history of vagrancy, which the magistrates must have taken into account when they sentenced her to two months' hard labour.[6]

Any estimate of crime based on quasi-official statistics, therefore, is almost certainly an undercount and many people in the nineteenth century were contemptuous of men like Dr Colquhoun, who argued authoritatively from 'evidence' drawn from the statistics. Nevertheless, whatever deficiencies they contained, the statistics are there and they form part of the evidence about the period, but with due caution being exercised at all times.

In England and Wales, crime statistics started to be collected from the courts and the associated hotchpotch of local bodies responsible for law enforcement by the year 1810. However, it was not until the mid-1830s that official government figures, collected mainly from the courts, were published. These were organised into six main categories: offences against the person; offences against property, involving violence; offences against property, not involving violence; malicious offences against property; offences against the currency; and miscellaneous offences.

In 1856, three additional categories were included, reliant upon information provided by the newly reformed police forces. These were: indictable offences notified to the police; the number of individuals convicted and imprisoned; and committals for trial on both indictment and before summary jurisdiction.

The Select Committee on Police (1853) bemoaned the absence of reliable statistics on crime and criminals. Their report concluded:

> There are from 11,000 to 20,000 persons constantly in the criminal gaols, of which number a large proportion of persons known as living wholly by habitual depredation. From evidence deduced we find that in rural gaols they have been engaged in crime longer, whereas in gaols in boroughs, where there is paid and trained police, they are engaged in crime for shorter periods before capture. The police information as to the number of crimes committed, which is inferred from the extent of crimes judicially pursued and punished, is widely erroneous.

In support of their conclusions, the Commissioners drew upon evidence from both the police and members of the public. For example, Thomas Burt, a commercial traveller, reported that he travelled extensively throughout the country, and when asked where he considered the most dangerous part, he replied:

> … of my own knowledge I may state that the districts which I and other travellers feel the least comfortable travelling are the neighbourhoods of the northern manufacturing towns, as in the vicinity of Manchester, where some ferocious highway robberies have been committed. In the immediate neighbourhood of Manchester, I am aware they have a police, but I am not aware of the existence of any in the other places.

Robert Orrell testified on behalf of manufacturers in Lancashire and spoke of their insecurity and fear of being violently attacked when travelling the local highways. He said that he never used the road to Blackstone Edge or Todmorden because 'people there are barbarians to an unusual degree'.

Deputy Constable J.S. Thomas and Superintendent Davies of the Manchester police were among those who bore witness to the problems associated with the police, crime and reliable statistics in large towns in the 1830s: 'There was a special need for public security in these excited districts,' said Mr Thomas. 'The business of excise collection was especially dangerous. The Customs Officers were beat-off, notwithstanding their sabres, with showers of stones by the Irish.'[7]

Whilst the Commissioners' report raised some concerns regarding incidents of public disorder associated with Chartist activities, the real driving force behind their report's conclusions was the threat to middle-class property and business interests caused by incidents of robbery, and by larcenies of finished goods and raw materials transported to and from manufacturing districts on public highways and canals.

Terms such as crime, criminal and police were bandied about in the nineteenth century just as loosely as they are today. Seldom do we have any precise definition. When people in the nineteenth century spoke of 'criminals', for example, they usually meant that class of people who lived a life of their own, separate from the rest of the community, who were usually easily distinguished by their clothes and habits. What is now known as 'white collar crime', carried out by clerks or fraudsters employed at the margins of a respectable trade or profession, rarely entered the debate. Criminals were seen as Dickensian figures like Fagin, Bill Sykes, the Artful Dodger and their ilk. Crime was what they did and what they lived by. Members of the 'criminal class' were not the only ones who committed crimes, but they had adopted a way of life in which crime played an important part, and to a great extent they could easily be identified. Whether or not these definitions are valid today is not really the point to be considered; the contemporary evidence has to be considered in its own terms, and these nineteenth-century definitions and understandings are the ones denoted when the term 'crime' and 'criminal' are used.

Another word frequently used when discussing 'criminals' is the word 'juvenile'. The people of the nineteenth century can be forgiven for using it loosely for it can seldom have been possible to prove the age of any youngster brought before the courts who sought deliberately to obscure the facts. Compulsory registration of births was not introduced until 1837, and thus it was not until the 1850s that birth certificates would have been available for the purpose of determining whether someone qualified as a juvenile. Therefore, in the judicial system, people had to rely on the appearance of a

young person, or his/her truthful declaration of age. This problem of identifying the age of juveniles troubled authorities across the country. The chaplain
of the Clerkenwell gaol, Rev. J. W. Horsley, reported as late as 1887:

> We take very little notice of names and ages in prison. Thus, Frederick Lane,
> aged 15, has just been sentenced to eighteen months for a first offence. He
> has previously been in custody as Alfred Miller aged 15, John Smith aged 16,
> John Collins aged 16, and John Keytes aged 17.[8]

The numbers of deserted, orphaned and runaway children and juveniles
roaming the streets of Manchester presented the police with a particular problem. Estimates of their number show that, from May to September 1835, 471
children were reported to the police as lost or missing. Over the same period,
only 138 were found and returned to their parents or to the workhouse. For
the years 1832–35, Manchester police counted a staggering 8,650 deserted
children. In the year 1843, police returns show forty-six apprehensions for
criminal offences committed by children under the age of 10; 525 by children
aged between 10 and 15; and 2,000 by children aged between 15 and 20.[9]

The high birth rates and death rates of the nineteenth century inevitably
led to a high proportion of young people in the population. There were not
sufficient jobs for all these youngsters and no schooling in the first half of
the century, other than that occasionally provided by Sunday schools. Their
parents were poor, worked long hours, and in many cases were spending what
free time they had in public houses and beerhouses. Moreover, the Poor Law
workhouses were unable to provide accommodation and relief sufficient for
all children in need. Consequently, many youngsters had to find a living as
best they could, which usually meant going out on the streets to beg, steal or
engage in prostitution.

Overall, the situation did not change until the second half of the century,
when the economy and job opportunities improved and when schooling
became compulsory for 5–12 year olds, following a succession of Education
Acts in the 1870s. A direct consequence of this legislation was the removal of
large numbers of children and juveniles from the streets of Manchester, with
the result that membership of criminal gangs and individual criminal behaviours were significantly reduced.

Just like the wider society, Manchester's criminal underclass was hierarchically structured. At the top of the heap sat the swell mobsman, who could so
easily be mistaken for a gentleman or 'dandy' as he regularly loitered in the
streets around the Exchange and in the vicinity of banks and clearing-houses

in the town centre. Often in league with a younger boy, he would walk into a bank and take up a pen and begin to write on loose paper. He would continue to watch the movements of unwary customers collecting money at the counters. In case he aroused suspicion, he would have already armed himself beforehand with a cheque on another bank to use as a 'blind'. If stopped he would plead ignorance, claiming that he had entered the wrong bank. He would continue to wait to see into which pocket the customer put his money, and then he and the boy would follow their victim into the street where often other members of the team were now waiting. The boy would give a signal and his accomplices would confront the victim, often using force, and with comparative ease steal the money and any other valuables, before running off with the proceeds of their crime.

There was a kind of fraternity of swell mobsmen who would meet and exchange ideas and stories of their exploits. The reporter Angus Bethune Reach described their activities and haunts when he wrote: 'There is a tavern in Blakely Street, now known as Charter Street, with a coloured lamp like that of a doctors, called the Dog and Duck. This is the house of call for many of the swell mobsmen of Manchester and the most superior class of prigs [thieves].'[10]

Thieving was a specialised job; the stealing of a gentleman's handkerchief by a 'buzzer', for instance, required a different technique from 'thimble screwing' or stealing a pocket watch. Shoplifting was considered a skilled and lucrative craft that was much on the rise as more and more stalls and shops opened on the main thoroughfares. Less prestigious, but on the increase, were the 'sneaksmen', who stole goods in transit from carts, barges and carriages.

The fences, or receivers, of stolen goods were well-respected members of the criminal fraternity. A well-known and esteemed fence, called 'one-eyed Dick', lived in a shop off Oldham Road. Another was Joe Hyde, landlord of the London Tavern in the centre of town.

Whilst it may be claimed that a distinguishing feature of the criminal class was that they had chosen not to follow the path of respectability – hard work, sobriety and self-help – there were those whose personal circumstances made them quite unable or incapable of making choices with positive outcomes, leaving them at the mercy of exploitation by inscrutable villains of the worst kind. For example, the town of Manchester suffered from a major vagrancy problem, particularly beggars soliciting alms from passers-by. Many of them claimed that they were ex-soldiers who had served their country against the French and had been injured on the battlefield. They were joined by others who were infirm or who had been injured at work, often exhibiting their wounds or injuries to arouse pity. Moreover, it was common practice for

vagrants to pay 'rent' to members of the criminal class for a part of the pave-
ment considered a lucrative pitch.

Manchester's Detective Chief Inspector Caminada recalls that there
were criminal gangs still operating around the streets and alleys of central
Manchester well into the second half of the century:

> Gangs of well-known thieves could be seen loitering at street corners dis-
> coursing over their doings and many a hard fight they waged with the police
> who did not always come off without serious injury. In this part also the
> sharpest of 'crossmen' [thieves] congregated; men who could pass muster in
> a crowd always well dressed and plenty of money to spend. There was no
> difficulty in getting rid of the proceeds of their robberies as Joe Hyde, Bob
> McFarlane and Patsy Reardon, three notorious fences, were always open to
> take their illegal gains, while 'Cabbage Ann' and 'One Armed Kitty' were
> keepers of establishments the fame of which was known to the vast majority.
> 'Coshers' were another kind of criminal who preyed on the community. They
> got hold of some girl whom they compelled to lead a loose life, and when she
> had accosted and decoyed her victim to some convenient place, the 'Cosher'
> would put in an appearance and rob him of all the valuables he possessed.[11]

Reports of bodysnatchers operating in and around Manchester served to
terrify whole neighbourhoods in the early nineteenth century. Also known
as 'the resurrectionists', these despicable characters disposed of resurrected
bodies through third parties acting on behalf of members of the medical profession. One such third party was known as Captain Sellars, no doubt because
of his smart appearance rather than his rank. He claimed his customers were
medical researchers from the Manchester hospitals.

William Chadwick, Chief Constable of Stalybridge at the time, wrote in his
memoirs how extensively the practice was carried on in the Manchester district:

> On January 15th 1828 the body of Mrs. Hall was stolen from the chapel
> yard at Hollinwood. On December 20th 1830, the body of Joseph Ogden
> was stolen from the same place. The same year, the body of Mrs. Booth was
> stolen from the chapel yard at Denton. In this case, the exhumed body was
> afterwards recovered under a heap of soil near to Debdale Lane, Gorton. It
> was supposed that the body had become so decomposed as to be of no use
> to doctors or medical students. On February 11th in the same year, a child
> of nine weeks old was interred in a grave in the chapel yard at Gorton, in
> which a Mr Thomas Dunkerly aged sixty-two years had been interred on

April 15th the previous year. Five weeks after the interment of the child (on March 17th) Mr Aveyard, the Sexton, noticed the gravestone out of order and found the 'resurrectionists' had been during the night and taken the coffin of Mr Dunkerly and the child. The general opinion in this case was that the snatchers had come from the Audenshaw district.[12]

The practice had virtually ceased by the 1840s and Captain Sellars became so reduced in circumstances that he worked for a while at the gasworks as a general labourer, and he died very poor and some say very miserable.[13]

On examination of apprehensions made by the Manchester police for the year 1843, a disproportionate number of those arrested were found to be women. Out of a total 12,147 apprehensions, no less than 3,658 were women. Many of these were engaged as prostitutes, often working in concert with pimps and thieves, but not wholly averse to working alone whenever the opportunity presented itself. Robbery and pickpocketing were the commonest forms of criminality with which prostitutes were associated. 'Most of the girls will rob by violence and especially drunken men,' reported Ellen Reece, an inmate at the Salford gaol. 'Prostitutes were known to practise picking clients' pockets while their trousers were down and then we would run off while his disarray hampered pursuit.'[14]

There were 330 known brothels and 701 common prostitutes in Manchester at this time, according to the Chief Constable's report for 1843. These figures are low in comparison with those at neighbouring Liverpool, which reported 520 brothels and more than 2,000 prostitutes. The conditions in these premises were so appalling that when members of the Constabulary Select Committee visited houses of ill-repute in Liverpool in 1837, they found them to be 'creeping alive with vermin and the women just lying like pigs, doing nothing, dressed in gaudy clothes, torn and soiled with blood and dirt, the effects of drunkenness and quarrelling. In this respect, Liverpool has become one of the most notorious centres for prostitution outside London.'[15]

The writer Leon Faucher sought to provide an explanation for Manchester's low prostitution figure, and in so doing caused outrage amongst the local womenfolk. He wrote: 'Prostitution for money has little scope amongst the inferior classes where clandestine connections are so common and where chastity, instead of being the rule amongst the females, tends to become the exception.'[16]

This view was contested by Angus Bethune Reach, who defended the morality of Manchester's factory girls when he wrote:

The fact is, as I am assured, that there exists among the mill girls a considerable degree of correct feeling (sometimes, indeed, carried to the extent of a saucy prudery) upon these subjects. They keep up a tolerably strict watch upon each other, and a case of frailty is a grand subject for scandal throughout the whole community. There appears, however, to be no doubt whatever that prostitution is rare among the mill girls. In the Manchester penitentiary in 1847, the number of female inmates who had worked in mills amounted to only one third of the number who had been domestic servants.[17]

Of the total 12,147 apprehensions, 4,198 were for drunkenness. What worried contemporaries most, however, was the understanding that drunkenness led to all manner of crimes, especially those involving violence. Evidence that drunkenness was often a precursor of crime was provided by Dr Hudson when he appeared before the Select Committee on Public Houses in 1857. He claimed: 'One fifth of all crime in Manchester arises from drunkenness.' He was supported by the chaplain at Preston gaol, Rev. Clay, who reported: 'I find that at least 35 per cent of all crime must be put down to drinking in beer houses and public houses.'[18]

Detective Chief Inspector Caminada also believed that drink was a major contributing factor in criminal behaviour in Manchester:

Around Deansgate in the 1870s, are such places as the Dog and Rat; the Red White and Blue; the Old Ship; the Pat McCarthy; The Green Man, and other equally notorious places which were then in full swing as licensed beer houses. Passing these places, the pedestrian's ear would be arrested by the sound of music proceeding from mechanical organs, accompanied sometimes with drums and tambourines. On entering the premises he would find a number of youths and girls assembled in a room furnished with a few wooden chairs and tables. The women generally lived upon the premises, the proprietor of the den often adding to his income by the proceeds of their shame. There were also well known beer houses which did nearly the whole of their business during prohibited hours, with all sorts of poisonous stuff being sold to the public under the guise of beer and spirits. Men were employed by the licensee for the purpose of watching for the police and warning of their approach.[19]

Manchester's public houses and beerhouses grew in number during this period, as residents of damp, overcrowded dwellings sought the warmth and relative comforts provided, as well as the liquid refreshment. What is often overlooked is just how beneficial and significant public houses were in poor working-class districts at this time, often providing a venue for community meetings and gatherings of all manner of associations. For example, many workmen were forced by their employers to meet in a designated public house in order to collect their wages, which would often be paid to one trusted employee in a large sum so that he was obliged to cash the sum of money across the bar and then divide it into smaller proportions for distribution. Usually, the employer and the publican would share the profits which followed such practices.[20]

In 1843, there were 502 public houses and 781 beerhouses known to the police in Manchester. Under the terms of the Beer Act of 1830, beerhouses were restricted to only sell beers. This piece of legislation was a deliberate attempt by the government to wean members of the working class away from gin drinking, which had become a serious problem. It allowed anyone who had a spare room and could afford a few shillings (usually eight) for the licence to legally sell beers to the public. The problems associated with gin drinking were far more prevalent in large seaports like London and Liverpool than in Manchester. Unlike public houses, the police did not supervise the beerhouses. Consequently, the local magistrates were virtually powerless to stop the rapid escalation in their numbers. In the ten years up to 1853, the number of beerhouses in the town rose from 781 to 1,572, an increase of 791. By contrast, the number of public houses actually fell during the same period from 502 to 484.

Dr James Kay, Manchester's Medical Officer of Health, viewed drunkenness as a serious moral collapse leading to all manner of criminal behaviours, and strongly opposed the terms of the Beer Act. He wrote:

> The decency of our town is violated even in this respect, that every street blazons forth the invitations of these haunts of crime. Gin shops, taverns and beerhouses encouraged by law, and over which the police can at present exercise but an imperfect control, have multiplied with such rapidity that they will excite the strong remonstrances which every lover of good order is prepared to make with government, against the permission, much less the sanction, of such enormities.[21]

It was not until the 1870s that effective controls over the selling of alcohol and its consumption were introduced. In 1872, the government reacted to the 'state of drunkenness' in towns across the country by passing a Licensing Act, which empowered Justices of the Peace and the police to regulate the sale and consumption of alcohol in all licensed premises: 'All ale houses, gin palaces and premises selling alcohol are required to be licensed by the local justices, who themselves must be wholly satisfied that the premises and the applicant are fit and proper for the purposes declared.' Drunkenness in public places became a summary offence and, if accompanied by such aggravating features as disorderly behaviour or being in charge of a carriage, horse or sheep, carried a power of arrest and an appearance before the magistrates.

The effectiveness of this piece of legislation can be gleaned from Caminada's own observations:

> I am glad to say that I have aided, during the last twenty years, in putting an end to over 400 such places as those I have described. For a number of years a most determined course of action was pursued by the police, and one by one the beerhouses and public houses in which lawless characters of the worst type nightly assembled were deprived of their licences. One cannot compare the present and past state of the city in this respect without recognising the wonderful improvement which has been effected.[22]

Official criminal records of the courts and police in this period show that larceny, robbery, burglary and assaults featured as the most common breaches of the law. However, those crimes known as fraud and embezzlement rarely found their way into the criminal returns or court records of the day. In 1865, *The Times* published a leading article on the case of a Mr Payne, treasurer of the Manchester Relief Fund, who had pocketed £2,400 from the funds. It noted how Payne had avoided prosecution because the law was 'simply not geared to cope with such a middle class offence. The legislation regarding embezzlement applying only to junior clerks and servants'.

Inequality in the law was recognised by writers such as Alexis de Tocqueville, who wrote:

> When some have great wealth and others nothing, it is necessary that the arm of authority should be continually stretched forth and permanent laws or regulations made which may protect the property of the rich from the inroads of the poor. Laws and government may be considered in this and in every case as a combination of the rich to oppress the poor and preserve to themselves the inequality of the goods which would otherwise be soon destroyed by the attacks of the poor.[23]

In his assessment of the judicial system that operated in the nineteenth century, Reiman wrote:'In such an unequal society the rich get rich, the poor get prison.'[24]

In the nineteenth century, private property had become sacrosanct, elevated in law almost to the level of a deity. Social historian Douglas Hay describes how the ruling class 'set new standards of legislative history, passing act after act to keep the capital sanction up to date and to protect every conceivable kind of property from theft or malicious damage'.

Inequality in nineteenth-century society and its impact on criminal behaviour became a hotly disputed topic. For example, in 1816 Robert Owen put forward the view that a lack of 'property' was a principal cause of crime. He stated:'If the poor cannot procure property, and are not supported, they must commit crimes or they will starve.' However, Owen's view was not widely shared. In 1839, the Royal Commission on a constabulary force concluded that crime was not caused by want 'but by the superior attractions of a criminal life'.[25]

The Commission's chairman was Manchester-born Edwin Chadwick, who wrote the report almost single-handed. Their findings were criticised by S.E. Finer, who claimed that Chadwick used a 'smokescreen of evidence' as a means of re-presenting his proposals for police reform which had been made in 1829. This criticism appears to be a little wide of the mark, however, as Chadwick's report was based on direct evidence provided by witnesses, many of whom were members of the criminal class, including burglars, robbers and prostitutes, as well as victims of crime, drawn from both rural and urban districts.

Any analysis of a connection between poverty and criminality must begin by making a distinction between crimes committed by those who were already members of the criminal class and crimes committed by those hitherto honest but who, through changed circumstances, had succumbed to temptation. Evidence suggests that people of honest habits would have to suffer the greatest of hardships before they descended into committing crime. Edwin Chadwick and his Commissioners were of the opinion that 'if a man was honest by the time he was twenty then he was honest all his life'.[26] Chadwick concluded:

We have investigated the origin of the great mass of crime committed for the sake of property and we find the whole ascribed to one common cause, namely the temptation of the profit of a career of depredation as compared with the profits of honest and even well paid industry. The notion that any

considerable proportion of the crimes against property is caused by blame-
less poverty or destitution we find disproved at every stage.[27]

There was also a well-informed body of opinion which argued that any connection between economic depression and crime could be misleading, and
is shown in so many instances to actually work in the reverse. Crime was
thought to increase in good times, largely because of the amount of drink
consumed by those enjoying the fruits of full employment, and, as drink was
considered a precursor of crime, so the incidence of criminal behaviour went
up as increasing quantities of alcohol were consumed.

In support of this argument, Matthew Davenport Hill, Recorder of
Birmingham in 1875, wrote:'In the manufacturing districts a flash of prosperity
which suddenly enhances the rate of wages overwhelms the working classes
with temptations to indulge in liquor, a cause of crime which is more potent for
its increase than the diffusion of plenty is for its diminution.'[28] The link between
prosperity, drunkenness and crime was identified by a number of contemporaries including Rev. J. W. Horsley, a London prison chaplain.[29]

No doubt there were those working men who stole a little here and there
without being detected and who succumbed to temptation during hard
times, but the evidence provided by contemporaries suggests that, on the
whole, honest people remained honest despite great hardship. This view was
reinforced in the last quarter of the century by Detective Chief Inspector
Caminada, who observed:

> We came across men, women and children who followed no regular call-
> ings and who as yet were not members of the criminal class. A poor English
> artisan out of employment has too much pride and independence of spirit
> to go begging, he would prefer to suffer in silence with the help of neigh-
> bours and the pawnshop than so degrade himself; and, at the last extremity
> he knows there is a person as a relieving officer on whose assistance he has
> a just and honest claim.[30]

Frederick Engels argued that criminality among the poorer sections of society
was not a moral issue but a consequence of the social and economic conditions created by capitalism:

> Capitalism pitchforks the new proletariat, often composed of immigrants from
> pre-industrial backgrounds, into a social hell in which they are ground down,
> under paid or starved, left to rot in slums, rejected, despised and coerced, not

only by the impersonal force of competition but by the bourgeoisie as a class, which regards them as objects not as men, as labour or hands.

The Capitalist supported by bourgeoisie law imposes his factory discipline, fines them, causes them to be jailed, discriminates against them and imposes the Malthusian Poor Law of 1834. Progressive industrialisation and urbanisation forces them to learn the lessons of their social situation and in concentrating them, makes them aware of their power as a social class.

The workers face their situation in different ways. Some succumb to it, allowing themselves to be demoralised; but the increase in drunkenness, crime and vice is a social phenomenon, the creation of Capitalism, and not to be explained by the weakness and shiftlessness of individuals. Others submit passively to their fate and exist as best as they can as reasonable, law-abiding citizens, taking no interest in public affairs and thus actually helping the middle class to tighten the chains which bind them.[31]

Frederick Engels' classic work, *The Condition of the Working Class in England*, is drawn largely from his experiences of living and working in Manchester during the 1840s. He went on to collaborate with Karl Marx to produce *The Communist Manifesto* and they both became major exponents of socialist ideas right up to the present day. Engels was born in 1820 in the Rhineland town of Barmen, Prussia (now Wuppertal, Germany), and arrived in Manchester in 1841, after spending a year in Berlin with the Prussian Guard Artillery. Before his arrival in Manchester, he spent some time in Cologne, where he met Karl Marx (who was editor of the *Rheinische Zeitung*) and started a life-long friendship and collaboration. It was in this period that he became a staunch communist, and was already writing articles proclaiming that capitalism was in its final stages and a working-class revolution in England was inevitable.

When he arrived in Manchester, Engels found workers facing one of the most devastating economic slumps of the century. It was not unreasonable that he should believe that Manchester was entering the final stages of capitalism, and that some form of revolution was imminent. We now know that this was the prelude to a major period of economic expansion, partly based on the massive development of railways, and iron and steel, allied to textile production.

Engels went to work at his father's cotton factory, Ermine and Engels, located next to Weaste railway station, alongside the Manchester–Liverpool railway line. Known as the Victoria Mill, it employed 400 operatives. Among the operatives employed at the Victoria Mill were sisters Mary and Lizzie Burns, with whom Engels formed a close friendship. All of them lived together at No. 2 Walmer Street, in Rusholme; No. 27 Cecil Street; a house in Thorncliffe Grove; and finally a house in Dover Street, off Deansgate.[32]

Sociologist D.É. Durkheim supported Engels' analysis of the situation in Manchester, in part at least, in his 1893 classic, *Division of Labour in Society*. Durkheim concluded that during periods of rapid social change (such as occurred during the Industrial Revolution), traditional social controls, norms and rules broke down in the face of capitalist expansion, with the individual becoming confused and isolated. In this state of *anomie*, the individual was at risk of engaging in deviant behaviours and criminality. The many young migrants from the countryside, having escaped the social controls of family and community to enjoy the freedoms provided by new circumstances and acquaintances, would easily fall into Durkheim's state of *anomie*. The number of young migrants coming to Manchester from the countryside and from as far away as Ireland might well be considered a crime-producing factor.

Dr James Kay was particularly worried by this influx of young migrants that swelled Manchester's population:

> Some of the most savage exponents of criminality were not to be found amongst Manchester's indigenous poor but from migrants and especially those from Ireland. Drink was the Irish weakness and drunkenness often the precursor of crime. The effects of liquor on the Irish, in every depredation and murder needs only to be averted to; it is certain that the abuse of this destructive stimulus ferments and keeps alive the most atrocious and appalling crimes.[33]

Police action to apprehend Irish perpetrators of crime often resulted in serious outbreaks of violence. The superintendent of Manchester's night watch reported to the Constabulary Commission in 1839:

> It repeatedly happens that in order to apprehend one Irishman in those Irish districts we are forced to take ten to twenty watchmen. The whole neighbourhood will turn out with bricks and stones. A man will resist by fighting and struggling in order to gain time till his friends collect for a rescue.[34]

Ironically, in the Manchester police of 1845, 25 per cent of officers were of Irish descent.[35]

A study of Irish immigrants and criminality in Lancashire, conducted by Dr W.J. Lowe, shows that of all prosecutions in Manchester in the year 1861, the number of persons who claimed to be Irish-born made up no less than

30 per cent of the total. In the port of Liverpool, the figure was 37 per cent, and in Preston 26 per cent.[36]

This situation was identified by the Constabulary Commission of 1839, which was set up to 'inquire into the best means of establishing an efficient constabulary force in the counties of England and Wales'. It reported:

> When large bodies of Irish of less orderly habits and prone to the use of violence in fits of intoxication settled permanently in towns of South Lancashire, the existing police force, which might have been sufficient to repress crime and disorder among the purely English population, has been found under these altered circumstances inadequate to the regular enforcement of the law.[37]

The steady flow of Irish migrants into the manufacturing townships increased greatly in the mid-1840s as a result of the Great Famine. By 1851, the Irish-born accounted for 17 per cent of the Manchester population, compared with 7 per cent in Ashton-under-Lyne, 10 per cent in Stockport and 10 per cent across Lancashire. Many were concentrated in the poorest districts, such as Ancoats, where 36.8 per cent of the population was Irish.[38]

Manchester was not alone among the manufacturing districts in experiencing problems associated with drunkenness among the Irish-born population. At neighbouring Oldham, for example, the local newspaper – the *Chronicle* – reported on 30 May 1868:

> We regret to say that a feeling of animosity between the English and Irish sections of our population manifested itself by overt acts of outrage on Monday evening. The beating-up of an Oldham man by a gang of Irishmen has led to mobs numbering as many as 1,000 strong attacking both St. Marys and St. Patricks churches and the nearby Postman's Knock beerhouse in Lord Street. The watch committee held an emergency meeting on May 26th and authorised the issuing of cutlasses to the police.

Contemporary reformers recognised that if life was to be made safer, more sober and more prosperous, the underlying causes of criminality needed to be addressed with some urgency. Positioned at the top of the reform agenda were religious worship, education, self-help and co-operation, all aiming to tackle what they perceived as being the main causes of crime: namely ignorance, drunkenness and poverty.

Many among Manchester's working class found support and fellowship through religious worship. Most of the population, of whatever social rank or background, attended religious services at least once a week, on a Sunday. Society in the nineteenth century cannot be understood without reference to the religious mindset of its people.

Though the Church of England was always the main provider, dissenting groups gained more followers in the century after 1750. The Church of England failed to meet the religious needs of Manchester's rising Christian population made up of Baptists, Congregationalists, Nonconformists, Presbyterians and Methodists. Roman Catholics formed just a tiny minority of Manchester's population at the start of the century but gradually, as the number of Irish migrants increased, so too did their congregations.

Religious pluralism was to be found throughout society. During the first half of the century, Nonconformity chipped away at the dominance of the Anglican Church. For example, between the years 1773 and 1851, the number of Nonconformist congregations in Manchester increased tenfold, with forty dissenting chapels being built. By contrast, in the year 1830 Manchester had just sixteen churches and three chapels servicing its Anglican congregation; the only churches to be built at this time were St George's in 1798 and All Saints' in 1820.

The Anglican Church was already forfeiting its traditional position as the 'church of the people', as more and more people in towns like Manchester came to associate it with the dreaded Corn Laws. Recognising that special measures were needed, the Church belatedly created a Manchester diocese in 1847 and appointed James Prince Lee to be its first bishop. His episcopate was marked by the creation of 163 new parishes across the borough. Undoubtedly, this wave of church-building and restoration on such a grand scale made a contribution to the development of a respectable, conformist, law-abiding section of the working class, through its reinforcement of such values as obedience, decency, sobriety and good manners.

The Roman Catholic Church's congregation soon formed a numerous community, swelled by the number of Irish migrants and, to a lesser extent, Italian migrants. In the last quarter of the eighteenth century, just one small Catholic church was located in Smithy, next door to the Grey Mare public house in Ancoats. By the turn of the century, there were new Catholic churches in Rook Street and Mulberry Street, followed by St Augustine's Church in Granby Row, which was built in 1820.

It is believed that Jewish traders in the Exchange and surrounding shops met regularly at rented premises off Deansgate, in the area now known as John Dalton Street, where a synagogue was recorded around 1750. The first purpose-built synagogue was built in nearby Halliwell Street in 1825.

The Methodists were becoming more numerous in Manchester, with nine chapels operating by 1820. The central chapel in Oldham Street, its most prominent, was erected in 1780. Another five chapels were built by 1824, to service a body of worshippers from the Wesleyan Methodists, such as the Independent Methodists and the Methodist Connexion.

However, for observers like Engels, religion was little more than the 'opium of the masses', inculcating middle-class values that would subdue the working class into believing that the fruits of their labour were to be rewarded in heaven and not on earth. What was often overlooked, however, was that in addition to Sunday services, many churches provided Manchester's poor children with basic reading and writing skills. For example, in 1825 the combined number of scholars receiving a gratuitous education at Thomas Henshaw's Bluecoat School, and the Collegiate and Catholic schools, was 2,582; by comparison, the number of Sunday school scholars was estimated at 25,684, a figure which amounts to five-sixths of the total number of children aged between 5 and 15 estimated to live in Manchester at this time.

Bamford describes how children at his local Methodist church in neighbouring Middleton were taught to read and write extracts from the Bible: 'At the beginning and at the close, hymns were sung and prayers took place. It started at 8.30 a.m. and after a break for lunch recommenced in the afternoon up to 4 o'clock. Boys and girls attended and it was regularly crowded.'[39]

Believing that all Sunday schools were entirely altruistic, however, would be a mistake. Initially, at least, nothing was more calculated than the way some Church schools indoctrinated the children of the labouring poor to keep them in a constant awareness of their station in life. The Commissioners appointed in 1861 to enquire into the state of popular education in England received the following evidence from the Rev. James Fraser, later appointed Bishop of Manchester:

Even if it were possible, I doubt if it would be desirable with a view to the real interests of the peasant boy, to keep him at school till he was 14 or 15 years old. But it is not possible. We must make up our minds to see the last of him at 10 or 11. We must frame our education upon this hypothesis; and I venture to maintain that it is quite possible to teach a child soundly, in a way that he shall not forget all that is necessary for him to possess, by the time he is 10 years old.

G.M. Trevelyan summed up this view when he wrote: 'The new charity schools and Sunday schools had the merit of trying to do something for all, but they had the demerit of too great an anxiety to keep the young scholars in their appointed sphere of life and train up a submissive generation.'[40]

Notwithstanding this qualification, the expansion of Sunday schools represented the beginning of popular education, an education that was free to the scholar. As such, it made an important contribution to raising many members of the working class out of ignorance and providing a potential for self-improvement.

Significantly, in terms of preventing crime and disorder, religion became an important vehicle for carrying ideas of temperance in the 1830s and '40s. 'Signing the pledge' became for many as though they were undergoing a religious experience. Drink was seen as a major factor in explaining poverty, criminality and vice among the urban poor. It was therefore recognised that to entice men and women away from the comforts of the pub and beerhouse, there needed to be put in place alternative cultural and leisure attractions such as libraries, Mechanics' Institutes, and train journeys to the countryside or seaside – all of which were supported by the temperance movement.

Blackford, however, in *The Church in Cottonopolis*, championed the socialist approach, pointing out that the gospel of sobriety had its limitations and bowed to the gospel of low wages, harsh living conditions, sickness and loss.[41]

Whilst it is difficult to estimate just how influential the temperance movement was, it is widely acknowledged that it became one of the pillars of respectability at the same time that public houses and drunkenness flourished. Sadly, moral exhortation only appealed to the few. The many continued to support the pub and partake in the culture of drink.

The artisan's passion for improvement through education did not diminish during this period, however. We find voluntary learning centres opening up across Manchester, with movements such as the Mechanics' Institute, Hampden Clubs and the Co-operatives all providing reading rooms and newsrooms where men and women could attend and read, or have read to them, newspapers, periodicals and all kinds of books. There can be no doubt that education and religion came to play a significant part in influencing the knowledge, aspirations and behaviour of members of the working class, considerably more so than has been previously recognised.

Adult education came to the fore when, in 1824, a small group of middle-class reformers, led by Benjamin Heywood, a Manchester banker, founded one of the first Mechanics' Institutes, whose aim was to help artisans and mechanics learn about the application of science to manufacturing. The founding fathers included William Fairbank, the famous engineer; Thomas Hopkins, a local politician; and Richard Roberts, the mechanical inventor, who had agreed among themselves each to contribute the sum of £10 to the scheme and to prevail on others to do likewise. Their first meeting was held on 7 April 1824, at the Bridgewater Arms, and they constructed the first purpose-built Institute in Cooper Street on 14 May 1827 at a cost of £7,000.

Heywood, in particular, became increasingly concerned for the moral and social welfare of Manchester's working class and he refocused the aims of the Institute towards education and elementary studies. Reading rooms, with libraries and newspapers provided, were set up across Manchester, and its membership extended beyond artisans to include clerks, labourers and warehousemen. Membership rose from 379 in 1825 to 1,392 in 1838 (when the Lyceum was established), and by 1844 it had reached 2,096.[42]

Further expansion in its functionality saw the establishment of a savings bank in 1850 for the benefit of members and their families. Though undoubtedly beneficial to the working class, the movement was not initiated by them but by prominent middle-class reformers. Many of the original directors were members of the Nonconformist chapels at Cross Street and Mosley Street, and they came to view the major social and technological changes taking place in Manchester as an opportunity to reduce ignorance and poverty and encourage working men to help themselves.

However, not all members of the middle class were enthusiastic about educating the adult poor or their children. Some believed that it would most likely produce dissenters and radicals, which in turn could destabilise society. In 1828, Charles Knight reported that he found it extremely difficult to interest Manchester mill owners in the work of his charity, the Society for the Diffusion of Useful Knowledge, and in 1844, Frederick Engels reported that he found his fellow middle-class manufacturers 'so recklessly stupid and smug in their blind egoism they do not even take the trouble to instruct the workers in their own bourgeois moral code'.

The justices at Strangeways prison were also found to be unenthusiastic about the idea of educating the poor. They commented: 'The present education system in prison is little better than a waste of time and money. No satisfactory result can be expected.'[43]

Whilst religious worship and the education of the poor manifestly improved the knowledge and self-worth of many, it was viewed by some socialists as having a most detrimental effect on their evolutionary potential. French historian Élie Halévy, intrigued by the contrast between the revolutionary tradition in France and the lack of radical success in England, argued that the different trajectories of revolution in both countries could be attributed to the spread of Methodist values among the working class in large towns.

According to this view, Methodism and its Sunday schools stifled the potential for protest and revolutionary ideas in manufacturing towns like Manchester.[44]

In the nineteenth century, when times were hard and individuals found themselves incapable of working due to old age or ill health, they went reluctantly to the parish for relief and support rather than engage in any form of criminal activity. Manchester's Churchwardens and Overseers of the Poor were found to have adopted a most sensible and sensitive approach in supporting their needy inhabitants, according to the visiting Commissioners looking into the administration of the Poor Laws in 1833. They wrote:

> The system of visitation at the abodes of the poor, so indispensable to a right disposal of cases in large towns, is brought to a great perfection here. Relief is never refused without visitation and each visiting overseer having a limited district acquires an accurate knowledge of the conditions of the poor, it is part of his duty to be present at the board sitting for relief and to assist in regulating the amount. The cases of applicants for relief are carefully considered at the boards and disposed of as it appeared to me with discrimination and liberality.[45]

Based on the principle that pauperism was predominantly a moral lapse rather than an economic one, Lord Sidmouth's parliament passed the Poor Law Amendment Act in 1834, which sought to de-pauperise the 'lazy, shiftless, able-bodied poor' by making it a condition of relief that the recipient must enter the workhouse, 'a place which must be made uninviting so that a pauper's situation would always be less eligible than that of the lowest independent labourer'.

As it turned out, however, the Act was not particularly relevant to towns like Manchester, where in times of economic depression, whole industries and communities would be thrown out of work temporarily. Moreover, as the Commissioners pointed out, poor relief dispensed by Manchester's overseers and churchwardens was reasonably efficient, and not 'ramshackled' or 'disorganised' as the Speenhamland System had apparently been when operated in the southern agricultural counties upon which the new Poor Laws were based.

In practice, the administration of poor relief in Manchester following the 1834 Act differed little from what went before. As soon as trade picked up, demand for labour, especially non-skilled labour, quickly absorbed the able-bodied unemployed.

The feared lock-ups in the 'Bastilles', and the splitting-up of families in the dreaded workhouses, did not really materialise in Manchester. The continuation with the old system had the effect of easing the minds of the working class (especially handloom weavers) who were fast becoming the main recipients of relief. Thus, Manchester's workhouses continued operating as almshouses for the sick, the aged, young children and the temporarily unemployed. Indeed, young children in the Manchester workhouses received an elementary education and were taught writing, reading and plain sewing for four hours each week in addition to one hour spent in church.

It was the considered view of the churchwardens at the time that a supportive, responsive system of poor relief also had the effect of preventing criminal behaviour by those whose plight had pushed them literally to starvation levels.

The early workhouses in Manchester were located at the upper end of Deansgate (known as 'the dole'), with another at New Bridge Street, which was opened in 1793. Records of 1793 describe 'a large, spacious, elegant building near to the conflux of the Irk with the Irwell'. (The MEN Arena now occupies this land.)

Demands for relief were considerable right up to the 1850s and beyond. At New Bridge Street in 1849, the Guardians decided to set up an industrial workhouse at nearby Tib Street, 'to provide more employment for inmates', and it became so successful that very soon afterwards they were renting a mill in Ancoats for use as another workhouse.

By 1858, it was decided to sell the New Bridge Street buildings to the Lancashire & Yorkshire Railway Company for extensions to be made to their Victoria station. With the proceeds, they went on to build a new modern workhouse in Crumpsall, North Manchester, the site of the North Manchester General Hospital. The new workhouse provided accommodation for 1,660 inmates, made up of 745 able-bodied, 152 women (including 76 with infants), 248 'idiots, imbeciles and epileptics', 255 children under 16 years of age, 200 sick, and 60 'probationers'. The Crumpsall site was extended several times in the 1870s and '80s, recording a daily average of 1,025 inmates.[46]

Industrial benefactors, such as Sir Benjamin Heywood, became involved in many schemes and initiatives to improve the lives of the labouring poor. In one example, in 1845, Heywood was so moved by the plight of his tenants occupying a block of terraced houses in Miles Platting that he set up a range of schemes for their direct benefit. These included a public baths and washhouse (with twenty-three private baths and forty-eight washtubs also provided), a day school, Sunday school and a savings bank. What marks out Heywood as atypical of benefactors of the age is that most of his tenants were handloom weavers or cotton mill operatives, and in no way were they dependent on him as their employer.

One of the most outstanding self-help schemes promoted in this period was the co-operative movement, which had its origins in the 1820s and 1830s as part of a wider socialist vision. Inspired by Robert Owen and his New Lanark mills experiment, Manchester's radicals, such as Elizabeth Dixon and E. T. Craig (both veterans of Peterloo), advocated the creation of co-operative communities in which members would have an equal share in the ownership and control of food production and distribution. By the early 1830s there were eleven such societies in and around Manchester, and it was Manchester which hosted the first ever Co-operative Conference in 1831, at which fifty-six societies were represented.

This form of idealistic community vision gave way to a more pragmatic retail movement, with the very first Co-operative shop being opened by the Rochdale Pioneers in Toad Lane in 1844. The pioneers laid down a set of principles which involved a commitment to provide pure, unadulterated food; insistence on cash sales; dividends on purchases; a savings club; and democratic control. In addition, it was a declared intention that the society would promote sobriety through the opening of temperance hotels. By 1850, the retail movement was firmly established, with 150 branches providing grocery sales across the country.

Manchester soon emerged as the natural centre of the movement, and housed such major organisations as the North of England Wholesale Agency and Depot Society Limited in Crumpsall, which was renamed the Co-operative Wholesale Society (CWS) in 1863; the Co-operative Insurance Society (CIS) in 1867; and the Co-operative Union and the Co-operative Bank in 1877. By the end of the century, 4 per cent of the population of England and Wales were members of the Co-op, and sales amounted to 6 per cent of the retail trade in England and Wales.[47]

Membership of the co-operative movement helped to raise those members of the working class who so aspired to become 'respectable'. Alongside religious worship, education, liquor licensing and an improving economy, it helps to explain the reported reduction in crime and disorder during the second half of the century.

Attempts to divert members of Manchester's working class away from the pub and beerhouse, and to embrace more healthy pursuits, gathered apace during the period up to the mid-century. As early as 1833, in a letter to the Select Committee on Public Walks, Dr Kay identified the need for the provision of healthy alternatives when not in the workplace:

> The working classes of Manchester are ignorant of all amusements outside
> the very small portion. The few hours which intervene between labour and

sleep, are generally spent either in the tavern or in making necessary family arrangements. On Sunday the entire working population sinks into a state of abject sloth or listlessness or even into more degrading conditions of reckless sensuality.[48]

Joseph Fletcher, secretary of the 1840 Weavers' Commission, and Charles Mott, Assistant Poor Law Commissioner, both endorsed Dr Kay's commentary and highlighted the 'need for public walks and places of recreation'. Edwin Chadwick followed up these observations when he pointed out to the Select Committee on Public Walks that on 10 February 1840:

> ... extensive arrangements were made for holding a Chartist meeting and for getting-up what was called a demonstration of the working classes which greatly alarmed the magistrates. The police commissioner, Sir Charles Shaw, persuaded the Mayor to get the Botanical Gardens, Zoological Gardens, Museums and other public institutions thrown open to the workers and their families at the hour they were invited to attend the Chartist meeting.
>
> The Mayor undertook to be answerable for any damage that occurred from throwing open the gardens and institutions to the people that had never before attended them. The effect was that not more than 200 or 300 attended the Chartist meeting, which entirely failed, and scarcely five shillings worth of damage was done in the gardens or institutions by the workpeople, who were highly praised. A further effect was that the charges of drunkenness and riot before the courts were on that day less than the average of cases on ordinary days.[49]

With the era of trips to the seaside beginning in 1846, following the opening of the railway station at Blackpool, we find that in the Whit Week of 1848, 116,000 people left Manchester for Blackpool; and two years later no less than 202,000 set out on a day trip to the seaside. Many mill workers set up 'works' outing clubs' to save a shilling for the fare. The journey took over six hours. It was felt that the excitement generated by such trips and the very act of saving with workmates actually raised the moral standards and responsibility of the labouring poor.

Whilst it was thought that to get the labouring poor out of their unhealthy, smoke-filled environment and into the fresh air would improve their health and well-being, such initiatives were also driven by concerns generated by the widespread use of opium among the working class. It is widely known that working-class mothers in the nineteenth century made use of laudanum as a soothing, quietening drug for infants, often with fatal consequences. Berridge points out that, by 1840, medical societies were publishing reports voicing their members' increasing concern that the consumption of opium among the working class had risen to a frightening extent. For many, it would seem, opium was the first choice of medication when suffering stomach aches, toothache and sickness generally. It was a cheaper alternative to alcohol, which made it even more attractive during hard times.

It was de Quincey himself, who was among the first to present working-class opium use as a problem. In his *Confessions*, he wrote:

> Some years ago, on passing through Manchester, I was informed by several cotton manufacturers that their workpeople were rapidly getting into the practice of opium eating: so much so, that on a Saturday afternoon, the counters of the druggists were strewed pills of one, two, or three grains, in preparation for the known demand of the evening. The immediate occasion of this practice was the lowness of wages, which, at that time, would not allow them to indulge in ale or spirits.

He went on to point out that manufacturers preferred their workers to use opium rather than alcohol because they were less likely to be aggressive and more likely to arrive for work on time.[50] In 1849, Angus Bethune Reach also drew attention to the widespread use of opium among the adult working population of Manchester. One druggist told him:

> Laudanum, in various forms, is used to some extent by the adult population, male and female, and to a terrible extent for very young children. I sell about two shillings worth a week of laudanum, in penny worth for adults. Some use raw opium instead. They either chew it or make it into pills and swallow it.[51]

The risks involved in its use were not understood or appreciated at the time, but this was to change as medical professionals successfully pressed the government for restrictive legislation to be introduced. In 1868, the Pharmacy Act prohibited sales 'across the counter' in grocers' shops, allowing only professional pharmacists and chemists to stock and sell opium. As a result, the problem virtually disappeared in the last quarter of the century.

One of the most significant crime-prevention measures to be introduced in Manchester during the nineteenth century was the installation of street lighting. As early as 1807, Manchester's Police Commissioners began to manufacture gas and installed the very first burner or gas lamp above the police office, in suitably named Police Street, which is just off Deansgate. The chairman of the Commissioners recalled:

> I well remember the sensation which this lamp produced, and the crowds that night after night gathered in front of the police office to gaze at it, manifesting by their eager and intense curiosity a vague sort of impression that an element of nature was being developed that would be useful to mankind.[52]

By the end of the 1840s, electricity emerged as a rival form of lighting and once again a Manchester man was at the fore. In the evening of 7 August 1850, William Edwards Staite shone his electric light from the rooftop of the home of Manchester's mayor, John Potter, at Buile Hill, Pendleton. 'The rays of light were seen to have an intensity and brilliance far surpassing any other artificial light hitherto known.'[53]

Observers on surrounding hills, church towers and high buildings for miles around shared in the excitement. The scientist John Joule, watching from his home in Moss Side, 3 miles away, declared that he found the light 'most brilliant and beautiful'.

Surprisingly, very few orders for Staite's lighting followed, and electric lighting was barely heard of again until 1878, when a football match between Blackburn Rovers and Accrington Stanley was played in the evening under floodlights powered by Staite's electric lights. Inside the ground were 6,000 spectators and another 20,000 estimated to have gathered outside for a free view of the lights.

Without question, these inventions were to prove most effective as crime-prevention measures, making pedestrians feel safer, as well as assisting the police when they patrolled the streets and thoroughfares.

Whilst the coming of the railways greatly benefited Manchester's working class, an unintended and unforeseen consequence was that members of the criminal class also took advantage of this new form of travel, accessing towns far afield where they were not known, and enabling them to make swift getaways from scenes of crime and the pursuit of the police. Although criminality in the nineteenth century was overwhelmingly local, the railways opened up the country to the criminal and by so doing transformed the very nature of crime.

One infamous beneficiary was Charlie Peace, a prolific burglar and serial killer, whose notoriety was fuelled by stories of his exploits published in popular true-crime magazines.

Born Charles Frederick Peace on 14 February 1832, son of a Staffordshire miner, he suffered a serious leg injury when he was 14 which left him with one leg shorter than the other. He was described as being a 'small, ugly, lame individual, taken to be as much as twenty years older than he actually was'. Notwithstanding his physical deformity, Charlie Peace was known to dress very smartly and 'to move in a confident and open manner', claiming that in his experience the police did not suspect men who conducted themselves as gentlemen. In his pocket, he always carried a loaded revolver.

He was 47 years old when, on 25 February 1879, he was executed at Armley prison, Leeds, for the murder of Arthur Dyson, whose wife Charlie Peace had at one time hoped to marry. During his brief stay in the condemned cell, Charlie Peace confessed to murdering a Manchester police constable following an unsuccessful attempt to break into a house in Chorlton-cum-Hardy. Peace's revelation was all the more dramatic since a young man named William Habron had already been convicted of the constable's murder at the Manchester Assizes and had been sentenced to hang. Thankfully, the death sentence had been commuted to life imprisonment by order of the Home Secretary.

The murder of Constable 1015 Cock took place on the night of 1 August 1876. Constable Cock had paraded for duty that night at the Chorlton police station and was assigned to a beat covering Brooks Bar, on the boundary of Manchester. He was just 20 years old and had been in the police for eight months. It was on a triangular piece of land from which three main roads diverged – the Chorlton-cum-Hardy Road, Upper Chorlton Road and Seymour Grove – that Constable Cock was shot dead. A detached house in Seymour Grove had been burgled and the constable had walked up the drive to investigate when he was confronted by the escaping burglar and shot. Upon hearing the discharge of the firearm, Constable Beauland, who was patrolling a nearby beat, rushed to the scene and blew his whistle to attract attention. He was joined by two night-soilmen, who helped place Constable Cock onto their wagon and wheeled him to the nearby surgery of Dr Dill, where he died a short time later.

A thorough search of the neighbourhood was mounted for his attacker and, in a wooden hut, not far from the scene of the crime, the police discovered three brothers, William, Frank and John Habron, who were all known to them through previous encounters. Indeed, Constable Cock had only recently arrested all three of them for disorderly behaviour. The brothers denied any involvement in the murder or the burglary and claimed they were 'sleeping rough' in the hut because they had insufficient money to pay for lodgings.

Police evidence in the case turned out to be entirely circumstantial. Several witnesses came forward to testify that the brothers had been overheard in public houses threatening to avenge their arrests by attacking Constable Cock. In addition, William Habron was identified by a local shopkeeper as having spent some considerable time in his shop looking at guns and cartridges.

On their appearance before the Magistrates' Court, the charge against Frank Habron was dismissed because of insufficient evidence, but William and John Habron were committed to the Assizes to be tried before Mr Justice Lindley. Charlie Peace was to boast later that he was present in court through-out the two-day hearing and won the admiration of his neighbours in the public gallery for his 'expert knowledge of the law'.

The jury considered their verdict for two and a half hours before return-ing to find William Habron guilty of murder and John Habron not guilty. Donning his black cap, Mr Justice Lindley passed the death sentence on 18-year-old William, who shouted, 'I am innocent!' as he was led away from the dock to the cells.

Charlie Peace's condemned cell confession was accepted as being genu-ine, but only after a thorough investigation conducted by Lancashire's Chief Constable, Charles Legge. When he first met Peace, the Chief Constable did not believe his story as he thought he was 'courting further notoriety'. His mind was changed, however, when ballistic evidence, provided by a London gunmaker, showed that the bullet recovered from Peace's revolver matched that which killed Constable Cock. His report concluded that he was in no doubt that Peace was telling the truth.

It was subsequently revealed that following the conclusion of the Habron brothers' trial, Peace had travelled by rail to London where he went to live at No. 5 East Terrace, Peckham, accompanied by Mrs Thompson, his new mistress. He continued his unlawful profession as a burglar and opened an antiques shop as a legitimate cover, from where he would dispose of his ill-gotten gains. One evening in October 1878, Peace was engaged in burgling a house in Blackheath when he was observed by Police Constable Robinson, who arrested him as he was leaving the scene.

Once again, Peace produced his loaded revolver and shot the arresting con-stable in his arm. The officer was not seriously hurt and managed to hold onto him until his sergeant arrived at the rear of the premises. At the time of his arrest, Charlie Peace used the alias Mr Thompson. Subsequently, he was taken before the Assize Courts and convicted of attempted murder and burglary.

Whilst in prison, his true identity was discovered after Mrs Thompson claimed some reward money and told the police whom they had really captured. Peace was dispatched, under police escort, to Leeds to stand trial for the murder of Mr Dyson. On the train journey, Peace somehow managed to escape by throwing himself out of a carriage window, but he was soon recaptured by his guards and resumed his journey northwards.

Charlie Peace became famous nationwide, with his exploits being sensationalised in popular crime magazines of the time. He even appeared in Madame Tussauds' Edinburgh Wax Museum, where his notoriety was attributed to 'his unusual courage, and the notion that he was a kind of criminal gladiator, always pitting himself against authority'.[54]

To a certain extent, Peace's notoriety was further enhanced by a public statement from William Marwood, the public executioner, who carried out the sentence of the court at Armley prison. A newspaper reported that he said:

> A firmer step never walked to the scaffold. I admired his bravery. He met his fate like a man. I have never met a man who met his fate with greater calmness. On the scaffold, Peace grabbed my arm and said, 'God bless you. I hope I meet you in heaven.'[55]

Meanwhile, back in Manchester, the unfortunate William Habron, having been tried and convicted of Constable Cock's murder, was pardoned by the Home Secretary and received £800 compensation.

One of Peace's many admirers in the criminal fraternity was a burglar named John Jackson, a 24-year-old plumber, whose home was in Bradford. He was also known to the police as Edward Graham and Charles Woodfirth.

Jackson came to fame as being one of the very few prisoners ever to escape from Strangeways prison. He had arrived at the prison after being convicted of a burglary at the Salford home of Captain Poynter of the Salvation Army, and was sentenced to six months' imprisonment.

One afternoon in the summer of 1887, Jackson was called upon to use his plumbing skills at the home of one of the prison matrons who had previously reported a gas leak. Accompanied by a warder named Webb, Jackson set about repairing a faulty pipe in the kitchen. When he had finished the work, he took advantage of the situation and struck the warder a blow to his head that killed him. He then climbed out of a window and leapt over a wall before successfully making good his escape across Cheetham Hill Road.

He was on the run for several weeks before information was received by the Manchester CID that prompted Detective Chief Inspector Caminada to set out for Oldham, where two burglaries had taken place that appeared to possess the *modus operandi* of Jackson. One of them was at a house in Park Road, the home of Mr Taylor, who reported that an overcoat, jacket and pullover had been stolen. The second burglary was at the home of another Salvation Army captain, named Thomas Wood, who lived in Cromwell Street, Oldham. Enquires confirmed that a man of Jackson's appearance, who had been wearing an overcoat identical to that stolen, had been seen in local public houses, including the Jolly Carter in Lees Road. Somehow Jackson evaded arrest – and seemed to have moved out of the area altogether.

Similar burglaries were reported to the police at Wakefield, Wolverhampton, Stockport and Bradford, with Jackson taking full advantage of the rail network, before he was eventually recaptured and returned to Strangeways prison.

He was tried before Mr Justice Grantham and found guilty of the murder of prison warder Webb. A petition, with 20,000 signatories, seeking a reprieve for Jackson, was sent to the Home Secretary Henry Matthews, but he had no difficulty in refusing any commutation of the death sentence and Jackson was hanged on 7 August 1888.

Another prolific burglar operating in Manchester was Robert 'Bob' Horridge, who was born in Rochdale Road, Harpurhey, in 1849. Like Peace and Jackson, he too made use of the railways to carry out crimes and to evade police arrest.

Early in 1887, Horridge broke into the shop of Mr Angus Wood in Rochdale Road. At 4.30 a.m., as he was leaving the shop premises by a backdoor, he was confronted by a patrolling constable. He pulled out a revolver and shot the constable in his head but, before he could make good his escape, another constable, who had been alerted by the sound of gunfire, caught hold of Horridge. He too was shot, the bullet lodging in his chest. Fortunately, both police constables recovered from their injuries.

Detective Chief Inspector Caminada recalled searching the Manchester haunts of Horridge and receiving information that he had been seen boarding a train bound for Liverpool soon after the shootings. Accompanied by another officer, Caminada set off for Liverpool and spent some time searching an area in the vicinity of the railway station and the docks, before he spotted Horridge in Duke Street, standing outside the Prince of Wales public house. Armed with a police revolver, Caminada approached Horridge from behind and caught him by surprise. He wrote: 'I struck him a blow to his head with my revolver.' When searched, Horridge was found to be in possession of a loaded revolver. At his trial, he was found guilty of attempted murder and sentenced to life imprisonment.[56]

His arresting officer, Detective Chief Inspector Caminada, retired from the force in 1899, but continued to live in Manchester with his wife Amelia and daughter Mary. In 1907, he was elected as an independent member for Openshaw on the Manchester City Council. He died in 1914, at his home in Moss Side, Manchester, at the age of 70, as a result of injuries he had sustained in a bus accident in North Wales the previous year.

The next chapter takes a look at the effectiveness of the government's deterrence policy, which came to rely upon harsh and cruel punishments for its success.

Notes

1. S. McCabe, 'Crime', in D. Walsh and A. Poole (eds), *A Dictionary of Criminology*, 1983, p.49.
2. A.B. Reach, *Manchester and the Textile Districts in 1849*, 1849.
3. Minutes of the Select Committee on Police in Metropolis, 1816, p.63.
4. H. Mayhew and J. Binny, *The Criminal Prisons of London*, 1862, p.63.
5. Select Committee on Police, 1837, p.368.
6. British Parliamentary Papers Accounts and Papers on Deserted Children, 1836, Vol.41, p.23.
7. Select Committee on Police, 1837, p.47.
8. J.W. Horsley, *Jottings from Jail*, 1887, p.23.
9. British Parliamentary Papers Accounts and Papers on Deserted Children, 1836, Vol.41, p.23.
10. A.B. Reach, *Manchester and the Textile Districts in 1849*, 1849, p.54.
11. J. Caminada, *Twenty-five Years of Detective Life*, 1895, p.16.
12. W. Chadwick, *Reminiscences of a Chief Constable*, 1880, p.86.
13. Ibid., p.88.
14. J.J. Tobias, *Crime and Industrial Society in the Nineteenth Century*, 1967, p.106.
15. S.P. Bell (ed.), *Victorian Lancashire*, 1974, p.158.
16. L. Faucher, *Manchester in 1844*, 1844, p.41.
17. A.B. Reach, *Manchester and the Textile Districts in 1849*, 1849.
18. Select Committee on Public Houses, 1857, Vol.37, Question 3714 & 6104.
19. J. Caminada, *Twenty-Five Years of Detective Life*, 1895, p.20.
20. British Parliamentary Papers on Drunkenness, 1834, p.594.
21. J. Kay, *The Moral and Physical Condition of the Working Classes*, 1832, p.59.
22. J. Caminada, *Twenty-Five Years of Detective Life*, 1895, p.17.
23. A. de Tocqueville, *Journeys to England and Ireland*, 1868, p.78.
24. J. Reiman, *Ideology, The Rich Get Richer and the Poor Get Prison: Ideology, Class and Criminal Justice*, 1997.
25. Hay, D. et al., *Albion's Fatal Tree: Crime and Society in Eighteenth Century England*, 1977, p.22.
26. Chadwick papers, box 129, p.70.
27. Ibid., p.73.

28. M.D. Hill, *Suggestions for the Repression of Crime*, 1857, p.109.

29. J.W. Horsley, *Jottings from Jail*, 1887, p.57.

30. J. Caminada, *Twenty-Five Years of Detective Life*, 1895, p.15.

31. F. Engels, *The Condition of the Working Class in England*, 1844, p.12.

32. T. Hunt, *The Frock-Coated Communist*, 2009, p.230.

33. J. Kay, *The Moral and Physical Condition of the Working Classes*, 1832, p.45.

34. R. Swift, *Crime: The Irish in Britain*, 1989, p.88.

35. Ibid., pp.88, 178.

36. W.J. Lowe, *The Irish in Lancashire 1846–71*, 1975.

37. The Constabulary Commission Report, 1839, p.89.

38. J.K. Walton, *Lancashire*, 1987, p.253.

39. S. Bamford, *Passages in the Life of a Radical*, 1839.

40. G.M. Trevelyan, *English Social History*, 1967, p.196.

41. G. Blackford, *The Church in Cottonopolis*, 1997, pp.85–97.

42. M. Tylecote, *Mechanics' Institutes of Lancashire and Yorkshire Before 1851*, 1957, p.129.

43. M. Higgs, *Prison Life in Victorian England*, 2007, p.57.

44. É. Halévy, *A History of the English People in 1815*, 1987, p.45.

45. *Report from His Majesty's Commissioners for Inquiring Into the Administration and Practical Operation of the Poor Laws*, 1833, pp.260–365.

46. S. Hall, *Workhouses and Hospitals in North Manchester*, 2004.

47. G.D.H. Cole, *A Century of Cooperation*, 1945.

48. J. Kay, *The Moral and Physical Condition of the Working Classes*, 1832.

49. Select Committee on Public Walks, 1840.

50. T. de Quincey, *Confessions of an English Opium Eater*, 1822, p.31.

51. A.B. Reach, *Manchester and the Textile Districts in 1849*, 1849, p.28.

52. C. Aspin, *Lancashire: The First Industrial Society*, 1969, p.141.

53. Ibid., p.143.

54. M. Diamond, *Victorian Sensation*, 2003, p.183.

55. N. Storey, *Prisons and Prisoners in Victorian Britain*, 2010, p.198.

56. J. Caminada, *Twenty-Five Years of Detective Life*, 1895, p.260.

6

PUNISHMENTS

Early nineteenth-century England seemed to survive without an effective police force, through an over-reliance on its harsh criminal code and penal policy. In 1820, for example, there were 288 capital offences on the statute book. The threat of the death penalty was considered an effective deterrent and a means by which the political elite maintained power and control over the working class.

It was Robert Peel, as Home Secretary, who in the 1820s stated the government's intention to carry out a reform of the criminal law. He appointed a parliamentary committee, headed by James Mackintosh, to overhaul the existing system. The committee's proposals included repeal or codification of criminal law statutes and the abolition of capital punishment for all but murder and high treason. Peel's reform programme had less to do with mercy or humanitarianism, as some have claimed, and more to do with efficiency and the need for clarity. According to Douglas Hurd, 'Quite simply, Peel found the criminal law to be in a muddle and, as a born administrator, he found the task [of reform] appealing to his practical mind.'[1]

The task he had set himself would have been lost, however, unless something was done about the application and enforcement of the law. The reform of policing, therefore, became a logical follow-on from the reform of the criminal law, as we shall see in Chapter 7.

Through the course of the century, there was a discernible shift in government policy with regard to the punishment of those in breach of the criminal law. In the early years, punishment was often a public spectacle enjoyed by the masses. Execution by hanging took place outside of prison walls, usually on elevated scaffolding for all to see, and often accompanied by all manner of entertainments, including food stalls, jugglers and fortune-tellers. The condemned man would end up 'wriggling' on the end of a rope as he gasped for air only to be saved from further pain by friends and family pulling on his legs to hasten his death. This practice gave to the English language the phrase 'you're pulling my leg'. Being secured in the stocks or being ducked in the river also took place in the town's most prominent places so that others might be deterred from committing similar acts in breach of the law.

Demands for reform grew apace, with ideas and reports published by archcritics, including Jeremy Bentham, John Howard, and local reformer Thomas Butterworth Bayley JP, who argued for a more liberal prison system balancing the need for punishment with prevention and rehabilitation. The reformers successfully persuaded Peel and his successors of the gross ineffectiveness of the present system. Their most notable achievements were the Gaol Act of 1824; the Penal Servitude Acts of 1853, 1856, and 1863; the Habitual Criminals Act; and the Prevention of Crimes Act of 1871, which introduced prescribed fixed sentences for specific offences, a separation of the sexes, and probation at the end of long sentences to be supervised by the police.

Reformers relied to a great extent on the ideas of the 'classicist school', led by Cesare Beccaria, who called for a fairer, more efficient, legal and penal system to replace the old feudal model. Among the many flaws identified, Beccaria pointed out that safeguards against wrongful conviction were all but absent; existing laws were poorly drafted and vague; and judges were left with considerable discretion when deciding guilt or innocence. Significantly, Beccaria called for a definite fixed penalty for specified criminal offences, according to their gravity, which would replace the existing catch-all 'capital offence'.[2]

Changes to the penal code also reflected changes taking place in the wider society. For example, in a feudal, agricultural society, fines were not an option for the vast majority of wrongdoers as they were impoverished and resident in houses tied to the landlord. In a capitalist, industrial society, the majority of the labouring class was earning some form of money and living in rented accommodation, so that fines were a more appropriate punishment option for relatively minor offences.

In the Manchester of the early nineteenth century, wrongdoers found themselves punished by imprisonment in the house of correction or in the dungeon sited on the Old Bridge, bordering the city of Salford; by public whipping at the rogues' post; or by being confined for an indefinite period of humiliation in the stocks. Prostitutes, or 'notorious women', were ducked in the public pond by means of the ducking stool, which was situated in Market Street, close to where Piccadilly Gardens stands today.

The stocks stood in the Market Place next to Old Millgate up to 1812, when they were removed. A contemporary chronicler described the scene at the Manchester stocks:

> Noon, Saturday, 1812, being Market Day I saw the last man ever subjected to the punishment of the pillory, standing on a table, the object of jeers and 'chaff' of the country folk who had come into the Market Place. About the same time I also saw two boatmen in a cart in Deansgate, somewhere about the site of the present library, these men had been tapping a brandy cask en-route for London. They were roped to a triangle in the cart and received each, fifty strokes from the cat-o-nine tails.[3]

The dungeon consisted of two apartments, one over the other, and was housed in the middle pier of the triple-arched Old Bridge. Those who were unfortunate enough to be lodged in the lower dungeon were often in a most perilous situation from the rise of the river by floods.

Occupying a space between Hunts Bank and Chetham's School stood the house of correction. Built in 1581, it was originally known as the New Fleet, 'for the detention of rogues, vagabonds and sturdy beggars'. Inmates had to undergo a period of hard labour 'in order to instil them with a desire for hard and honest toil'. However, houses of correction, or bridewells, as they were sometimes called, were embodied into the Poor Law system and came to include the aged and infirm, who were classified as the 'deserving poor'.

The distinction between the house of correction and the gaol gradually vanished by the mid-eighteenth century, and the justices were allowed to commit a large number of offenders to either establishment as they saw fit.

By the end of the eighteenth century, a new modern prison was built in Stanley Street, Salford, named the New Bayley after Mr Butterworth Bayley JP, who had previously published a critical report on the conditions at the house of correction at Hunts Bank.

The first inmates were admitted in 1790 and each of the 150 prisoners had a cell to himself, which was an unknown luxury in the prison system at this time. A new female prison was opened in Rusholme Road in 1823, for women 'having deviated from the paths of virtue and desirous of abandoning their vicious courses and becoming qualified by virtue and industry, for reputable situations'. This exclusively women's prison was built in accordance with the recommendations made in the Gaol Act: that men and women must be housed in separate prisons.[4]

By the early part of the nineteenth century, the government favoured the transportation of convicted offenders overseas as an alternative to imprisonment or execution. Under the provisions of the Transportation Act 1784, the numbers transported reached a peak in the late 1820s, with around 5,000 convicts shipped out to Australia each year. Numbers started to decline in the 1840s and virtually ended with the introduction of the Penal Servitude Acts of 1853, '56 and '63. It is estimated that over 162,000 British and Irish convicts were transported to Australia at this time. When the last transportation ship, the *Hougoumont*, reached Australia in 1868, sixty-three out of the 280 convicts on board were recorded as being of Irish descent.[5]

Convicts sentenced to transportation were housed in one of eight hulks for up to two years prior to being shipped to Australia. The hulks were decommissioned naval vessels moored in the Thames estuary and off the south coast. They were replaced in 1821 by the newly built Millbank Penitentiary, on the banks of the Thames, near Westminster.

That the courts freely handed out sentences of transportation is evidenced in a section of William Rowbottom's diaries, 1787–1830. He wrote: 'October 24th 1814, opening of Manchester's Quarter Sessions Court, nineteen convicted persons (seventeen men and two women) sentenced to transportation for seven years.'

The registers of the hulks reserved for juvenile offenders serves to reinforce the view that such punishments were harsh and cruel by any standards. Thirty Lancashire youths were found to be on board the *Euryalus*. Two of them (15-year-old Matthew Carlisle and 12-year-old William Naylor) were sentenced to life imprisonment for housebreaking and stealing a cow respectively. Patrick Conway, aged 13, was serving fourteen years for stealing a brass bowl. John Murray and William Locklan, aged 12, were each serving ten years for stealing handkerchiefs.[6]

According to the Criminal Registers of 1838 (HO 27.55), 233 convicts from Lancashire were held in the hulks moored off Portsmouth and Chatham. Seven were serving life sentences and the remainder were serving terms between seven and fifteen years. Practically all of the sentences were for offences of larceny.

The wisdom of the day was that such harsh sentencing acted as a deterrent, whilst at the same time recognising that, due to the inefficiency of policing, the vast majority of wrongdoers would never be caught or brought before the courts for sentencing. The Penal Servitude Act was intended to replace transportation with a more humane approach, which included a new system of parole for prisoners who behaved themselves throughout their sentence. When they neared the end of their sentence, well-behaved convicts were granted a 'ticket of leave' authorising their early release under the supervision of the local police. Often this meant the discharged prisoner having to report periodically to the local police station to confirm his address and whether or not he was in work. In the 1880s, the number of discharged prisoners in Manchester who were placed under police supervision in any one year numbered around 1,000.

Whenever a prisoner was about to be discharged, he was provided with a new suit of clothes, either by the prison or by the Prisoners' Aid Society. One of the founders of this charitable association in Manchester was the governor of Strangeways prison, Captain C.W. Hill. Another leading member was Mr Thomas Wright, a local philanthropist, whose actions were singled out for praise by an ex-prisoner when he wrote to the prison chaplain at Preston:

> May I take the liberty of informing you of my gaining employment at the Leeds railway and it shall be my constant study to keep my place in an honest and sober manner. Sir, the kindness I have received from Mr. Wright, I would be ungrateful if I did not state it. He exerted himself in all places to get me work and provided me with money for the necessities of life.[7]

At this time, there was a noticeable softening in the sentencing policies of many judges on the Northern Circuit. Making use of their discretionary powers, judges preferred to substitute alternative charges and sentences on the indictment for those crimes that parliament had prescribed as 'capital offences'. Included in the list of capital offences were housebreaking, larceny to the value of £5, and horse, cattle, and sheep stealing. After 1815, as many as 95 per cent of convicted prisoners were pardoned from execution and sentenced to imprisonment or transportation as an alternative, which compared with 50 per cent in the previous thirty years. No one was executed in the North West of England after 1815 for crimes other than murder. Parliament finally abolished the death penalty for convictions other than for murder and treason under the Offences Against the Person Act, 1861.[8]

It was in the 1880s that William Marwood, the Home Office's hangman, invented the 'long drop' technique, which enabled the authorities to replace the public scaffold with a much more private affair operated behind prison walls. Marwood's 'long drop' involved a scientific calculation which included the condemned person's height and weight, and the precise positioning of the rope around the neck, all of which was designed to dispatch the condemned into oblivion in a fraction of a second.

However, not every 'long drop' execution proved a success. In 1885, at Exeter prison, John Ball, a 20-year-old servant, had been sentenced to hang for the murder of an elderly, wealthy widow named Emma Keys. He became the only man condemned to be hanged who survived three attempts at execution. On each occasion, Ball was hooded and placed on the trapdoors with a noose around his neck, and every time the hangman, James Berry, pulled the lever to activate the 'drop', the trapdoors jammed. After the third attempt, Ball was returned to his cell and the Home Secretary was contacted for further instructions. The message came back: 'Sir William Harcourt, Home Secretary, will commute the sentence to life imprisonment.'[9]

William Marwood regularly attended the Strangeways prison to carry out the sentence of the courts between the years 1874 and 1883. The Strangeways prison had been opened in 1868, as a replacement for the New Bayley at Salford. It was located in Southall Street, off Cheetham Hill Road, and was on the site of the old Strangeways Hall and Gardens previously occupied by Lt-Col Hanson and his family.

In a review of executions carried out at Strangeways, Fielding reveals that by the end of the nineteenth century the majority of prisoners executed for murder were of Irish descent and most of them claimed they were in a state of intoxication when they committed their crimes.[10] Examples include the case of 57-year-old Michael Kennedy, a local mill worker, who returned home in a drunken state on Saturday 5 October 1872 and shot his wife in the head after a quarrel. In another case, William Cassidy, an Irish immigrant, murdered his wife Rose on 9 November 1879, at their home in Rochdale Road, Harpurhey, on his return from the local public house. It was established that both parties had been drinking continuously throughout the day and became embroiled in arguments with their wives. Cassidy left the house only to return a short while later with a can of paraffin that he poured over his wife before setting her alight.

One of the few women to be hanged at Strangeways was Mary Ann Britland, a 38-year-old factory worker who lived with her husband Thomas at No. 92 Turner Street, Ashton-under-Lyne. Suspicions were aroused in the neighbourhood after Thomas died suddenly on 10 May 1886. Their 19-year-old daughter Elizabeth had also died suddenly just two months earlier. Notwithstanding these concerns a death certificate was issued and, after collecting the insurance money due, Mary Ann Britland went to live nearby with her friends Mary and Thomas Dixon. Just four days later, Mary Dixon died suddenly in great pain. A post-mortem was ordered and it revealed that she had been poisoned. The police started an investigation and the bodies of Thomas Britland and his daughter Elizabeth were exhumed, and again traces of poison were found.

Mary Ann Britland was arrested and charged with all three murders. She stood trial at Manchester Assize Courts before Mr Justice Cave on 22 July 1886, and was found guilty of all charges and sentenced to be hanged.

The day-to-day administration of summary justice in Manchester rested with the Justices of the Peace, the vast majority of whom were drawn from a recognisable pool of socially acceptable gentry families, reflecting the power structure in the country.[11]

A large majority of Manchester's magistrates fell into this category during the first half of the century, with the notable exception of Mr James Norris, the stipendiary magistrate, who was a salaried full-time official. Wealth acquired through manufacture or commerce remained second to land and inheritance when it came to public office, with members of the new middle class being excluded from a judicial role.

In 1820, the year following Peterloo, Manchester's justices all resided outside the town's boundaries, with just two exceptions. The bench consisted of: Robert Fielden of Withington Hall, Ralph Wright of Flixton, W. Marriott of Prestwich, Rev. C. Ecclestone of Smedley, James Brierley of Manchester, James Hibbert of Broughton Hall, J. Watkins of Bolton, W. Hulton of Hulton, J. Silvester of Chorley, J. Borram of Warrington, and J.T. Ridgeway of Ridgemount.

Included in the Municipal Corporations Bill of 1835 was a clause allowing the newly elected borough councils to appoint local justices from among their ranks of councillors. When the Bill passed through the Commons and reached the House of Lords, this clause had been removed. However, the Home Secretary, Lord John Russell, supported such a move, and for some years after was prepared to appoint those men whose names were submitted by the mayors of borough councils.[12] Here in Manchester, during the year 1840 for example, fourteen members of the local council, including the mayor, were appointed to the bench. This pragmatic approach adopted by Russell resulted in a fundamental change in the composition of the bench which benefited the local middle class at the expense of the Lancashire gentry. By the 1880s, Manchester's bench was made up of 80 per cent local industrialists, traders and merchants.

To sum up, we find barbaric forms of punishment much in evidence in Manchester at the beginning of the century. Gradually, the penal and judicial systems were reformed and replaced by a diverse range of measures considered more appropriate to the nature of the offence committed and the personal history of the offender. Middle-class reformers, including Mr Bentham, Mr Butterworth and Mr Bayley, pressured the government for a more liberal, humane prison system and succeeded in securing fundamental changes, which included single-sex prisons, separate juvenile detentions, and periods of probation at the end of sentences.

The human costs of such harsh punishments were high, with families torn apart and in most cases reduced to abject poverty. Government policy was a reflection of their fears that the working class were becoming out of control, as witnessed in France at the end of the eighteenth century. The popularly held view was that a strict adherence to a regime of harsh punishments for wrongdoing remained the most effective deterrent.[13]

By mid-century, a more confident and less fearful government was prepared to listen to the arguments presented by reformers, and came to recognise that repression and cruelty were hardly deterrents for the working class when only a pitifully small number of offenders were actually caught and punished. The second half of the century, therefore, was a triumph of humanitarianism, shaped by the ideas of Bentham and Howard, and introduced by Robert Peel as Home Secretary.

In the second half of the century, we find Manchester's magistrates' bench, previously made up of Lancashire gentry, now being replaced by a new order of middle-class industrialists, reflecting the changing power structures brought about by the modern industrial age.

Notes

1. D. Hurd, *Robert Peel*, 2001.
2. C. Beccaria, *On Crimes and Punishments*, 1764.
3. A. Darbyshire, *A Book of Old Manchester and Salford*, 1887.
4. E. Baines, *Lancashire*, Vol.2, 1824, p.145.
5. C. Matthew, *The Nineteenth Century*, 2000, p.99.
6. E.C. Midwinter, *Law and Order in Victorian Lancashire*, 1968, p.7.
7. M. Higgs, *Prison Life in Victorian England*, 2007, p.66.
8. P.J. Helm, *A New Portrait of England's Hanging Judge*, 1966, p.14.
9. M. Holgate and D. Waugh, *The Man They Could Not Hang*, 2005, p.4.
10. S. Fielding, *Hanged at Manchester*, 2008.
11. D. Foster, 'The Changing Social Origins and Political Allegiances of Lancashire JPs, 1821–51', PhD thesis, 1972.
12. S. Simon, *A Century of City Government*, 1938, p.61.
13. A. Brooke and D. Brandon, *Bound for Botany Bay*, 2005, p.13.

7

THE ESTABLISHMENT OF A PROFESSIONAL POLICE FORCE

By the early nineteenth century, it had become abundantly clear that the police – whether day or night police – were defective and shown to be so. Both the Court Leet and the Police Commissioners found themselves restrained by legislation in raising sufficient money to appoint and equip an efficient police force, had they wanted to. The right of the Court Leet to impose rates for 'general administrative purposes' had never been clearly defined and, after 1778, they could not even raise money for the payment of the Constables' Accounts, having to rely upon the generosity of the church-wardens paying out of the poor rate.

The Police Commissioners had the right to levy rates for the purposes defined in the local Acts under which they were incorporated (1796), but such police rates were restrictive and might not exceed 18*d* in the pound in any one year. Most of the townspeople, however, regarded these financial limita-tions as a valuable safeguard rather than as a constitutional defect. Indeed, the main objection to the idea of municipal incorporation was that a new bor-ough council might be far more extravagant than the Police Commissioners had been.

Even though a Committee of Inquiry, chaired by William Nield, had rec-ommended that 'a sufficiently numerous and properly organised police force was required to suppress recent instances of riot', the two bodies preferred to rely upon existing arrangements with neighbouring townships 'as relations were friendly and supportive'.

However, the standard of policing in neighbouring townships was no better than it was in Manchester. For example, the retiring Police Commissioner at Chorlton, Mr William Callender, wrote:

There was a case of a ratepayer whose house was robbed and who had called at the Chorlton Police Office every day for a week before he could get the assistance of an officer. On another occasion, the watchmen in the neighbourhood of Plymouth Grove were frequently found asleep within the porch of my house and following a family event, the departing guests had sometimes to step over these vigilant guardians of the peace. On one occasion, the superintendent found one there and took away his staff, lantern and hat without wakening him.[1]

Inefficient and ineffective the police in Manchester and its neighbourhood may well have been, but demands for some kind of reform to improve the situation were repeatedly dismissed by parliament following Committees of Inquiry reports in 1816, 1818, and again in 1822. In the final report of 1822, the committee's concluding paragraph read: 'The very idea of reforming the existing local system of policing is incompatible with British liberties.'

By 1829, however, circumstances were to prove more favourable for Robert Peel, the Home Secretary. Yet another parliamentary inquiry had reported on the 'policing problem' and provided the Home Secretary with a 'deluge' of facts and figures about the rise of crime in London in particular. The committee's report was to prove favourable to Peel, in that it argued that a better system was needed with some urgency and that it could be provided without necessarily costing more money and with no new restraints on personal liberties.

Armed with these recommendations, Peel set about preparing a new Policing Bill for parliament to consider. He also briefed the Duke of Wellington on the concerns previously raised over personal liberties: 'Liberty does not consist of having your home robbed by gangs of thieves and in leaving the principal streets of London in the nightly possession of drunken women and vagabonds.' He went on to skilfully use the public's fear of crime and becoming victims of crime as the main thrust of his argument for reforming the police. As a result, the Metropolitan Policing Bill successfully passed through parliament and became law in June 1829.[2]

The Metropolitan Police Act established a constabulary for London – except the City of London – with two magistrates appointed to organise and supervise the new force. Robert Peel appointed 46-year-old Charles Rowan, a retired army officer, who had served with Wellington at Waterloo, and

Richard Mayne, a young Irish barrister, to the new posts. The two magistrates were provided with offices in Whitehall, at the rear of which was a small piece of land known locally at 'Scotland Yard'.

From the very beginning, Peel recognised that if it was to prove successful and overcome the open hostility felt by large sections of the working class, the new force would have to depend less on its legal powers and force of arms and more on the quality and discretion of the men recruited. Writing to Rowan and Mayne, he stressed: 'All nominations for the police, as well as promotions from inferior stations, should depend exclusively upon the character, qualifications and services of the persons selected; and I am satisfied that you have, on offering your recommendations to me, acted rigidly upon that suggestion in every instance.'[3]

While public order generated fear among the political class, fear of crime, especially crimes committed in public places, was the main driving force behind Peel's policing reform. Affection for the old watchmen and the traditional rights of the Medieval Court evaporated when tested against these concerns in a changing urban setting.

It is a popularly held view that Peel's policing reforms were primarily in response to fears generated by the disruption caused by the Chartists. However, in the year 1829, Chartist demonstrations were limited and did not gather pace until around 1838 and beyond.[4] Of greater concern for Peel and the Tories were the crimes and acts of debauchery that undermined the confidence and dynamic of entrepreneurs, merchants and manufacturers, who complained bitterly that it had become a frightening experience to visit some of the growing towns like London, Birmingham and Manchester, where their business interests were being seriously damaged by such lawlessness, which often went unpunished.

Peel stressed the criminal object of his reforms when he wrote: 'It must be understood at the outset that the primary object of the police is the prevention of crime. I am convinced that the strict adherence to this principle must entirely depend on the efficiency and character of the new establishment.'[5]

For most working-class people, however, their experiences at the hands of watchmen, government spies, and the military, shaped their attitudes towards this new policing idea. To overcome this initial hostility, its architects strove to construct a distinctive organisational style and image, quite separate from what had gone before. Rowan and Mayne laid down a set of rules that emphasised that the new force would be a uniformed civilian body of men; they would be unarmed; they would rely on the same legal powers that all citizens shared; they would be accountable to the public they serve; they would be insulated from direct government control; their actions would be subject to the rule of law, enforceable through the courts; and all new recruits would be drawn from a representative range of working-class backgrounds to facilitate popular identification.

The new policemen soon attracted the nicknames 'Bobby' and 'Peeler' after their founder Robert Peel, and were kitted-out with a blue swallow-tailed coat with bright buttons, blue trousers and a tall hat. The helmet was first introduced in 1869 to protect the wearer from head injury. Later, it was stated that for them to patrol their beats efficiently, constables must walk at a measured pace, initially set at 3mph.

The Municipal Corporations Act of 1835 enabled large towns like Manchester to follow the Metropolitan example. The Act contained the general provision that:

> If the inhabitant householders of any town or borough petition His Majesty to grant them a Charter of Incorporation, it shall be lawful for His Majesty, by any such charter as he shall think fit, on the advice of his Privy Council, to grant the same, to extend to the inhabitants of any such charter, all the powers and provisions in this Act contained.

The 'powers and provisions' included the appointment of a Watch Committee, whose first duty was to recruit a Chief Constable to oversee a newly established police force.

Local reformers considered that these provisions constituted sufficient reason for supporting the Bill, and in a single day organised a petition signed by 22,832 inhabitants. The successful campaign was led by William Nield, Thomas Potter, John Edward Taylor and Richard Cobden. The receipt of the charter was hailed as a decisive victory for the reformers but this congratulatory mood was to prove premature. The *Manchester Courier* advised its readers to take no part in the forthcoming elections for a newly constituted borough council, and the old institutions of the Court Leet, the Police Commissioners and the churchwardens all denied the authority of a newly elected council.

As a consequence, the administration of the town was in danger of being reduced to chaos. Although the Act of Incorporation stipulated that the newly elected borough council must set up a Watch Committee 'to appoint a sufficient number of fit men who would be sworn-in to act as constables for preserving the peace by day and night and preventing robberies and other crimes', in reality, the existing day police and the night watch continued to act as before, their wages now being paid out of the poor rate and police

rate combined. The parties in possession of the lock-ups and other premises occupied and used by watchmen, including the arms and accoutrements
belonging to the town, refused to deliver up their possessions to the new
borough council.

As if to make matters worse, the increased activities of the Chartists in
Lancashire and Yorkshire were arousing strong fears of a serious breakdown in
public order. At the same time, the rising price of bread exacerbated the situation
and led both workers and bosses to demand that the Corn Laws be repealed.

The chaotic situation facing Manchester prompted the Home Secretary
to intervene and introduce, by default, a special Bill in the summer of 1839,
empowering the Crown 'to appoint a Chief Commissioner of Police for
Manchester and to establish a new police force in that borough'. In many
respects this embarrassing situation lent support to the recommendations
made by Edwin Chadwick in the Police Commissioner's report of 1839,
that the Home Secretary should take control of all borough police forces
rather than leaving them in the hands of elected councillors. In essence, what
Chadwick and his fellow Commissioners were recommending was the establishment of a national police force under the direct control of the Home
Secretary. The Home Secretary had rejected this recommendation in favour
of local control and accountability.

The new Bill (as amended) set down that the new Chief Commissioner for
Manchester would hold office for two years, by which time (so it was hoped)
the conflict and rivalry would be at an end. In the meantime, it was stipulated
that all other police bodies were to be disbanded, and no police rates were
to be levied, apart from those of the Commissioner, and that these would be
restricted to not more than 8*d* in the pound.

The Home Secretary turned to recently knighted Sir Charles Shaw
with a request that he take up the post of Chief Commissioner of Police in
Manchester. Sir Charles had returned to England in 1836 after retiring from
the army in the rank of Brigadier General. Born in Ayr, Scotland, he was a
single man when he arrived in Manchester in September 1839.

A similar situation to that found in Manchester had also arisen in neighbouring Bolton, where the Courts Leet of Great Bolton and Little Bolton
claimed that they were still the legal authority in the face of a Charter of
Incorporation, and threatened legal action against the newly elected borough
council. Officers of the Court Leet retained control over the lock-ups, forc-
ing the council to use gaols at Preston, Lancaster and Salford. Here too the
situation had become chaotic, and tensions were heightened when a group of
local Chartists set fire to the Little Bolton Town Hall.

The Bolton Borough Council petitioned the Home Secretary with a request that they be included in the Manchester Bill, and invited Sir Charles Shaw to take overall command of policing in the borough, in addition to his responsibilities in Manchester. Their request was granted and Sir Charles Shaw took charge of the Bolton police force with immediate effect, supervising the newly appointed Superintendent Simptom and Superintendent Baker, who took command of day-to-day policing.

It was evident that if the new Chief Commissioner's appointment in Manchester was to prove successful, he would have to demonstrate to those inhabitants who paid the police rate that his new force was operating efficiently – in other words, that it provided value for money. The Chief Commissioner's first impressions proved most unfavourable. He wrote:

> I found that both the brown and blue police gave much attention to certain properties, taking positions for the whole night close to the houses of certain individuals, and I invariably found that the property most carefully, may I say exclusively watched, was that of Police Commissioners or members of local public bodies, thus forcing one to suspect that the much famed system of self-government was in reality selfish government. In addition, the streets of the wealthy were much better watched and lighted than those inhabited by the poor. About the same time, it is noted that a policeman on duty in Hulme reported seeing two men fighting in a field opposite the end of Boundary Street. On closer inspection the two combatants turned out to be the chief of the police force in Chorlton and an inspector of nuisances for the same township.[6]

In another report, Sir Charles Shaw referred to the practice of local watchmen knocking-up the workpeople to get them to the factory on time: 'I found the workpeople of Manchester in the habit of paying sixpence a week each family to the old watch for calling-up in the mornings and immediately put a stop to it. However, employers complained of the interception to business, requesting a return to the usual custom.' With some reluctance, Sir Charles Shaw agreed to allow policemen to continue the watchmen's traditional practice of knocking-up the workers, but fixed it at a reduced rate of 2*d* a week, provided the employers deducted the amount from their weekly wages and paid it over to the police funds. Ultimately, the police were relieved of their difficulty by a small group of professional 'knockers-up', whose number gradually increased until they covered the town and its suburbs.

In some ways, the new police differed little under Sir Charles Shaw's leadership from the old order, which placed great strain on him to show that it was indeed providing ratepayers with value for money. Most of the new recruits were from among the constables and watchmen previously employed by the Manorial Court and the Police Commissioners. The superintendent of the night watch, Mr M.J. Whitty, was made Head Constable, and fifty-three watchmen were made constables in the new force. A total of 320 constables, four superintendents and twenty-four inspectors were appointed in the first twelve months. It was not altogether surprising, however, that those same individuals who had previously been labelled grossly inefficient were employed by the new force, as few men were prepared to work such long hours in often dangerous conditions for as little as 14s per seven-day week.[7]

The same situation was to be found in neighbouring towns where the old, inefficient police were recruited into the new police force. At Liverpool, for example, responsibility for law and order rested on three separate forces – a day police, a night watch and a docks police – with all of them being described as 'lazy, corrupt and inefficient'.[8] These three forces were incorporated into one borough force in 1841, under the command of a new Chief Constable, Mr Michael Whitty, who transferred from the Manchester police on promotion. Of the 360 men who made up the force, 114 had previously served in the Liverpool night watch.

The provisions of the Municipal Corporations Act were not adopted at Rochdale, which had been served by a day police under the Court Leet and a tiny group of night watchmen. The Police Commissioners had been formed under the town's Improvement Act and Mr Thomas Butterworth continued in charge of a dozen night watchmen.

At Oldham, they relied upon an Improvement Act of 1826, which empowered the Police Commissioners to appoint four constables and a small number of watchmen for the prescribed duties of 'preventing fires, murders, robberies, burglaries and felonies, other outrages, disorders and breaches of the peace'. Records show that the four constables were named Joseph Chadwick, James Chadwick, John Wrigley and Thomas Walton, and that they were required to provide cover for twenty-four hours a day, seven days a week.

In his first report, presented to the Manchester Borough Council in 1840, Sir Charles Shaw set out the total expenditure of his force:

(a) Return of the total amount of the police expenditure in the Borough of Manchester, distinguishing the several ranks and numbers thereof, and the pay and allowances of each rank:

1	Chief Commissioner	£700-0-0d salaried
1	Receiver	£250-0-0d salaried
1	Chief Clerk	£200-0-0d salaried
1	Surgeon	£50-0-0d salaried
1	Chief Superintendent	£260-0-0d salaried
4	Superintendents (each)	£180-0-0d salaried
8	Inspectors (each)	£100-0-0d salaried
4	Sub-Inspectors	£1-10s-0d per week
13	Superior Sergeants	£1-5s-0d per week
31	Sergeants	£1-1s-0d per week
295	Constables	14s-17s-0d per week

These figures relate to the six months between 17 October and ending 17 April 1840. Signed Charles Shaw.

(a) Return of the total expense of the force for the same period:

Ordinary Expenses

Pay lists	£8019-5s-2d
Stable expenses and forage	£64-1s-4d
Stationery and printing	£286-6s-10d
Coals for police stations	£90-2s-1d
Gas lighting	£140-3s-3d
Surgeon's expenses	£35-16s-0d
Rent of offices and police stations	£210-7s-4d
Salaries of Chief Commissioner, Receiver and Chief Officers	£1103-0s-9d
Incidental expenses at police stations	£273-11s-0d
Total	£10,222-13s-9d

Extraordinary expenses

Furniture and bedding	£558-0s-9d
Alterations to stations, lock-ups etc.	£583-8s-11d
Clothing	£2,569-14s-6d
Total	£3,711-3s-0d

Signed J.Thorpe (Receiver) and Charles Shaw (C.C.)

It is hardly surprisng that Sir Charles Shaw was subjected to heavy criticism from the parochial authorities, who made a critical attack on police admin-istration while at the same time emphasising that politics and cost were their over-riding concerns. Alarmed at the prospect of increasing costs being trans-ferred onto the police rates, they declared:

> … the sum which the Chief Commissioner already receives from the town of Manchester is at least £12,291 per annum, and that exceeds the cost of the day and night police when the management thereof was in the hands of the Boroughreeve and the Commissioners, and the force was then perfectly satisfactory to the public and was much more efficient than the force established and conducted by the Chief Commissioner of Police.[9]

Sir Charles was not prepared to stand idly by in the face of charges made by 'members of the old order' and responded accordingly:

> I am concerned at the various and vexatious difficulties which have been thrown in my way since my arrival in Manchester. The results of this opposi-tion have been to circulate reports of every possible nature, calculated to cause either a misapprehension of the measures I, from time to time, adopted, or to uphold them for public disapproval. Upon my arrival, I found two distinct police establishments, the numerical strength of these forces I found to be somewhere around 600 constables, under no general control and pos-sessing no inter-community of information, or any unity of action. The sum, however, expended upon these establishments I found to be around £40,000; while, on the contrary, the means at my disposal were limited at £16,052, a sum which it must be confessed is obviously inadequate.[10]

The council decided they would not become involved in this conflict, realis-ing that by this time Sir Charles Shaw's tenure was about to expire. With this in mind, therefore, in 1842, they petitioned the Home Secretary, Sir Charles Graham, that the validity of the charter had been established by due process of law; that the various bodies overseeing the police had now been absorbed into the borough corporation; and that the overseers of the townships had ceased to oppose the new council and were now prepared to pay the borough rates. The Home Secretary accepted the petition but insisted that the council 'give a distinct pledge that if the existing Act be allowed to expire they will forthwith take measures for the continuance of an efficient police so that peace and good order shall not be endangered'.

Unfortunately, at the same time as this exchange was taking place, the peace and good order of Manchester was threatened by working-class agitation and disruption. A series of plug riots broke out across the borough and in cotton towns across south-east Lancashire, when rioters sought to draw out the boiler plugs of the mills to immobilise them. This followed employers' threats to reduce the wages of textile workers, many of whom were already working part time.

The council called upon the military from the barracks at Hulme for protection, and it was reported that more than 2,000 soldiers, with at least six pieces of artillery, were deployed on the streets of Manchester in support of the police and special constables. Thousands of workers were reduced to 'utter wretchedness and despair', according to reports in local newspapers.

An alarmed borough council issued the following statement in the local press:

> Whilst deeply commiserating the distresses under which the working-classes have been for sometime past and are now suffering, it is considered to be of the utmost importance that the inhabitants should unequivocally and generally express their disapproval of the illegal and riotous proceedings by which this neighbourhood has been during the last few years disgraced. Aldermen and Councillors of each ward are requested to convene meetings of the respectable inhabitants who are to be urged to come forward for the purpose of being sworn-in as special constables.

Local businessman and Justice of the Peace, Mr Absalom Watkin, described an incident of violence which broke out in August 1842:

> The outrages of the mob continue, those who have been turned out joined with them and shops have been plundered in the town and money extorted. Message after message arrives for assistance. I am sent with Mr. Stuart and Mr. Higson to confer with Sir Charles Shaw. We found him at Kennedy's mill with about 150–200 men, and nearby nearly as many soldiers, taking, as he says, a military view of the matter and concentrating his force to be ready to move where it may be urgently wanted; the usual patrols are withdrawn from the streets and all left exposed. He objects to the scattering of his force. In the meantime, the gasworks at Goulden Street are attacked and the police stationed there are beaten. A police station in the neighbourhood is pulled down. Mr. Callender goes with some dragoons and rifles and disperses the mob to then occupy the gasworks. While this was going on, the mob proceeded in different parts of the town to turn out the hands at mills and workshops and in some cases to help themselves to bread from the shops.[11]

By 20 August, peace and good order had been restored to a great extent, at least according to the editor of the *Manchester Times*: 'While at a distance Manchester is thought to be in a state of siege, the whole town may now be traversed without a single act of violence being witnessed.'[12]

The validity of the Charter of Incorporation had by now been established beyond doubt, and all responsible parties in the town come to recognise the legitimate authority of the elected borough council. In practice it meant that elected councillors could freely enter the town hall building in King Street for the first time. Prior to this, the Police Commissioners had refused to give it up and this had led to the first Manchester Borough Council meeting having to be held in a nearby public house.

As for the Chief Commissioner, Sir Charles Shaw, he returned to live in Richmond, Surrey, with his new wife Louisa Hannah and their infant son Charles Martin, after completing three years in the post.

On 24 October 1842, the Watch Committee appointed Captain Edward Willis as Manchester's first Chief Constable. Born in Prescot, Lancashire, in 1806, the youngest of nine sons, Captain Willis was educated at Charterhouse before entering the army in 1826. He served in Ireland, Bermuda and Jamaica before his retirement in 1937. In 1839 he was unsuccessful in his application for the post of Chief Constable of Lancashire, but accepted the post of Assistant Chief Constable at a salary of £200. He took over the direction of the southern half of that force with its headquarters at Newton-le-Willows. The successful candidate for the post of Chief Constable of Lancashire was John Woodford.

On his appointment as the Chief Constable of Manchester, Captain Willis more than doubled his salary to £450, with an additional £50 expense allowance. His deputy was Mr Richard Beswick, former assistant to Sir Charles Shaw, who had been appointed to the post after the transfer, on promotion, of Mr Whitty to Liverpool.

The new Chief Constable declared that he would immediately set about 'improving the strength and efficiency of the force', while at the same time 'endeavouring to introduce a rigid system of economy'.

The minimum wage level for constables was raised from 14s to 17s per week, which had the immediate effect of attracting an additional seventy constables in the first three months. When Mr Willis first arrived, the strength of the force had fallen to 318 constables and by the end of his first year in office it had risen to 398 constables, which included eight matrons who were called upon to deal with women prisoners, whose numbers were increasing.

To illustrate the economy of the force, the council published the following tables:

(a)

Manchester Police Force	Strength	Pay	Yearly expense	Cost per man
1839–1842	328	7s–17s	£23,622	£72-0s-4d
1842–1843	398	17s	£23,036	£57-17s-7d

(b)

Police Forces	Population	Strength	Cost	Average Cost per Man	Cost per Head of Population
Manchester	235,139	398	£23,036	£57	1s-11d
City of London	140,967	543	£41,351	£76	5s-10d
Metropolitan	2,032,458	4,685	£289,322	£61	2s-10d

Not surprisingly, the ratepayers were delighted with these figures. A representative of the Watch Committee declared:

> The watch committee has deemed it expedient to prepare such a financial statement as will enable the Council and ratepayers to judge how far the advantages usually anticipated and especially in an economic point of view, have been realised; and the watch committee has much pleasure in directing attention to this part of the Chief Constable's report, as affording strong evidence that the inhabitants of this borough have good reason to feel satisfied that the management and control of the police has been transferred from the Commissioner to the watch committee appointed by the Council.

The following tables are taken from the Chief Constable's report for 1843, showing the classification of offences and the number of persons apprehended:

(a) Offences Against the Person

Murder	1
Manslaughter	11
Rape	3
Intent to Commit Rape	4
Bigamy	6
Child Desertion	1

Assaults	655
Assaults on Constables	417
Total	1,098

(b) Offences Against Property

Burglary and Robbery	128
Theft without Violence	2,256
Malicious Offences Against Property	187
Currency Offences	56
Attempted Suicide	11
Rioting	24
Gambling	190
Illicit Distillation	33
Misdemeanours	305
Breach of the Peace	725
Drunkenness	4,198
Desertion and Neglect	141
Disorderly Prostitutes	836
Other Vagrants	1,869
Miscellaneous Offences	90
Total	12,147

Concerned that the number of apprehensions made by his officers did not match the numbers convicted by the courts, and that this kind of discrepancy might be interpreted as an example of inefficiency, Mr Willis reported:

It will be seen that the total number of apprehensions during the year 1843 was 12,147, the discharges amount to 8,408, summary convictions 2,981, and committals for trial 758. It will also appear that the number discharged amounts to about two thirds of the whole number apprehended, but of these a large proportion are of parties charged with drunkenness in which cases – except when occurring in the township of Manchester – the magistrates possess no power to convict.

The Chief Constable went on to cite cases of disorderly conduct, such as assault and offences of a similar character:

... in which although the magistrates have not punished, the interference of the police in order to maintain order and preserve the peace has been absolutely required. Parties are often taken into custody on strong and just suspicion of having committed a felony, and although remanded in some instances for several days by the magistrates are ultimately discharged, not because of having been improperly taken into custody but in consequence of the police being unable to obtain some link in the chain of evidence to fully substantiate the charge. It also frequently occurs in robbery cases involving prostitutes that the prosecutors keep out of the way and will not appear in court for fear of disclosure.

Sir Charles Shaw reported that his force experienced similar difficulties associated with prosecutions when he was in office. In 1841, for example, out of 13,345 persons apprehended, no fewer than 10,208 were discharged by the magistrates and 142 were discharged at trials heard before a judge. Specially trained detectives, and the scientific support for investigating crimes, were not available until the final quarter of the century.

Soon after taking command of the force, Captain Willis witnessed another serious outbreak of public disorder, which on this occasion involved soldiers from the local barracks. Kidd reports:

In May, 1843, a large disturbance broke out in Ancoats when a group of off-duty soldiers became embroiled in a brawl with locals at a well known public house. The police arrived and the main protagonists were arrested and taken to Kirby Street Police Station. This led to an angry crowd surrounding the police station demanding the release of the prisoners. After a short while, the mob forced their way inside and attacked the police officers on duty. Throughout the night, disturbances broke out across Ancoats and in the following morning a protest march from Ancoats to Piccadilly attracted an estimated one thousand marchers. Soldiers from the barracks were called out before peace could be restored.[13]

An eyewitness account is provided by Phillip Wentworth in his *Recollections of Manchester*:

I remember the police station at Oldham Road, on Manchester's 'B' division, when it was wrecked by an attacking party of soldiers who came from the barracks in Tib Street to avenge what [they] regarded as an insult to a colleague. When the police were reinforced, I was a witness to the hand to hand fighting which took place between them and the soldiers across the broad road, when blood flowed copiously and both soldiers and police fell with stunning blows under the feet of the remaining combatants. Never shall I forget the fury of the Colonel of the Regiment as he rode up the highway with his sword drawn to disperse the rioters. He scattered them as a hurricane scatters the ripe fruit from an apple tree. In a few minutes not one red coat was to be seen. But the greater part of the aggressors were arrested and brought to justice.[14]

The incident caught the imagination of national newspapers such as the *Illustrated London News*. On 24 May 1843 the concluding paragraph of their report reads:

Following their dispersal, the mob went on a rampage through the town centre, with several police stations being stoned and a large number of policemen reportedly injured. One of those injured was Inspector Lipsett of the Kirby Street police station. The mob was swelled by numbers of out of work spinners, who only the previous week had been turned out by their employers and taken before the magistrates and charged with 'picketing and assembling in large numbers'.[15]

The Colonel of the Regiment mentioned in Wentworth's report was a Colonel Arbuttnot, officer commanding the 72nd Highlanders and the 15th Foot Regiment. After his deployment at Manchester, Colonel Arbuttnot tendered his resignation on his appointment as equerry to Queen Victoria.

By mid-century, Manchester's peace and good order benefited from an upturn in overseas trade and a return to full employment in textile manufacturing. Chartist activity was now in decline, and what outbreaks did occur were confined mainly to the satellite townships of east Lancashire. According to its Chief Constable: 'Manchester is generally a quiet and orderly town; and upon the occasion of the Queen's visit in 1851 we had no barriers and had very little trouble keeping order.' (Question 2896, Select Committee on the Police, British Parliamentary Papers 1853)

When asked by the committee about the number of recruits to the force, the Chief Constable replied: 'They are mainly agricultural people from Derbyshire, Cheshire, and Yorkshire. There is a waiting list now of about 25. Special constables were used in 1842 and 1848 to assist with outbreaks of disorder, but they are recruited from the better and middle-class of persons generally.' (Q 2927)

In 1857, having completed fifteen years as Chief Constable, Captain Willis retired from the force to take up the newly created post of Inspector of Constabulary. He was the third inspector to be appointed, after John Woodford, the former Chief Constable of Lancashire, and Major General William Cartwright JP, a veteran of Waterloo.

The Inspectorate system was established by Lord Palmerston to try to gain some measure of control over the large borough police forces. In return 'for the right to inspect', the government offered local authorities a percentage grant of the running cost of the force.

Once again, however, Manchester Borough Council positioned itself in the vanguard of those local authorities which strongly opposed the government's 'unwarranted interference' in the privileges and independence of established boroughs. On this occasion, their protests proved to be successful and the government's proposed legislation was withdrawn. But this proved to be a temporary measure, and two years later the Bill was resurrected and passed through the necessary stages in parliament with few amendments, before being placed on the statute book.

The Inspectorate was required 'to secure the goodwill and cooperation of local authorities', and have 'a reliance on judgement, temper and discretion'. Their immediate task was to appraise the state of efficiency of the 237 separate police forces in England and Wales, and to pay the limited exchequer grant to those they certified as being efficient in point of number and discipline.

Woodford took charge of the Northern district, which included Manchester; Cartwright took charge of the Midlands; and Willis took the Southern district, which included the Metropolitan Police.

In his first inspection report, Woodford was most impressed with the state of the Manchester force: 'It consisted of 522 officers and constables and was composed of a remarkably fine and efficient body of men, most of them in the prime of life and health.' One of the tests of efficiency applied by the Inspectorate was the ratio of police to population. The County Police Act of 1839 imposed a maximum of one constable per 1,000 people, a figure well in excess of Manchester's ratio of one constable per 540.

Very few of the police forces in the Northern district were to meet this 'test of efficiency' or be reported on quite as favourably as the Manchester force. Woodford reserved severe criticism for those parish authorities 'with lock-ups insecure and non-existent guardians of prisoners'. In Northumberland, some lock-ups were so remote and isolated, and the police so indolent, that it was reported: 'Prisoners had been put in the lock-up sober and taken out drunk.' In some of the smaller boroughs, he found 'no police officers at all and no records kept of the prisoners taken in'.

At Rochdale, he was most unimpressed by the standards of behaviour displayed by some members of the force. He reported that three of their constables had recently been sacked for misconduct: 'Constables Fowler, Leary and Twist had been found guilty of abusing and threatening Alice Roberts in the Three Crowns Inn, one of them going so far as to thrust his head up her petticoats.'

At Wigan, he reported that when the borough council had agreed to establish a police force in the town, they were unsure of the precise numbers to be appointed and invited Constable Thomas of the Manchester force to advise the Watch Committee accordingly. He recommended that they set up a force of not fewer than forty men – but after careful deliberations over the costs involved, the committee decided that six police officers would be sufficient.

Thirty-five applications were received by the Watch Committee, who determined that only those applicants who were residents of Wigan would be considered. The position of Chief Constable was handed to John Whittle, who was considered eminently suitable as he was born in Wigan, lived in Wigan and had previous police experience in Wigan. All of the remaining five posts went to Wigan men, born and bred. The first to be appointed was Hugh Fegan, whose uncle, Richard Fegan, chaired the Watch Committee. Among the applicants who were turned down by the committee as being unsuitable, were a superintendent from the Manchester police, a sheriff's officer from Derby, a Deputy Constable from Pendleton, a constable from the Glasgow force and a constable from the Liverpool police.

The records show that Constable Fegan proved to be a man of questionable character and not really up to the job. After just a few weeks in the post, he was admonished by the Mayor of Wigan because his prisoners tended to become 'more intoxicated on their appearance in court than when put in the cells'. His final mistake was in 'making false entries in the station record books', a breach of regulations for which he was discharged.

At Oldham, the local council was criticised repeatedly by the Inspectorate for its failure to reach the standard ratio of police per population figure. As a consequence, the Home Secretary withheld the police grant year on year until 1870. Between the years 1856 and 1863, the strength of the force varied between fifty and fifty-nine constables. To meet the 'standard', this figure would have had to increase to seventy-two constables, based on the population estimate in the 1861 census.

The borough council's response to criticism from the Inspectorate was to state: 'It is not expedient to increase the police force at present.' It is ironic that by missing out on the Home Office's policing grant, they were actually costing the ratepayers more money. The fifty-nine constables in the

Oldham police force cost local ratepayers £3,658 per year, whereas the cost of seventy-two constables would have been £4,421. With the government's grant of 25 per cent, or £1,105, the annual saving for Oldham's ratepayers, had the council increased the number of constables from fifty-nine to seventy-two, would have been £342.

Similar to many other small forces, Oldham's police force had its fair share of disciplinary problems within its ranks. Records show that on 28 September 1855, Constable William Meek was disciplined for misconduct after 'having sold a cock which was given to him after it was found trespassing in a garden in Salem, Lees'. Constable John James Brooke was eventually dismissed on 8 November 1859. First of all, he had been reported for 'taking indecent liberties with a married woman'. Three days later he was reported again for 'taking indecent liberties with the daughter of Inspector Winterbottom'. Finally, on 8 November, he was 'found asleep whilst on patrol', and so ended his career in the police.[16]

The Inspectorate was particularly impressed with the welfare provisions in the Manchester police. Constables contributed 5d per week to the force's superannuation scheme. If, after fifteen years' service, a constable was forced to retire because of disablement, he could reckon upon a pension of at least one third of his salary, and upon a higher rate after completing twenty years' service. Retirement pensions for constables were by no means universal. At neighbouring Ashton, for example, no pension was paid, no matter how long the service completed by its constables.

After acknowledging the outstanding examples found at Manchester, the Inspectorate drew up national guidelines for the payment of pensions to all retiring or injured constables across the country. However, despite the sound arguments put forward in support of these provisions, the Home Secretary was not moved to instruct local councils in this matter and so this hotchpotch situation continued for the rest of the century.

Following the departure of Captain Willis, the Watch Committee decided to appoint Captain William Henry Palin as its Chief Constable. Born in India, Captain Palin was educated in England up to the age of 16, when he enlisted in the 17th Bombay Native Infantry. He subsequently became adjutant, paymaster, quartermaster and interpreter before resigning his captaincy and returning to England in 1856. Twelve months later and he was appointed the Chief Constable of the Manchester City police force. (Manchester became a city in 1853.)

There is little doubt that Palin's background and experience in the army proved attractive to Manchester's councillors, who continued to place value for money at the top of their policing agenda. In this respect, Captain Palin's appointment was to prove most satisfactory. By 1866, the Chief Constable

reported that the forces' income exceeded its expenditure by as much as
£2,597 10s 8d.

The entire annual cost of the force was £65,000, made up as follows:
the Chief Superintendent's salary was £600; the police surgeon, £500; the
receiver, £350; the superintendent was paid a weekly wage of £4 18s 6d; two
senior inspectors were each paid £3 6s 7d; twelve inspectors were each paid
wages ranging from £2 11s 3d to £3 1s 6d; fourteen station sergeants and
fourteen detective sergeants each received £2 1s; twenty-eight sergeants were
each paid £1 14s; and twenty-eight second-class sergeants were each paid
£1 11s 9d weekly; 296 constables received £1 8s 8d; 165 constables received
£1 5s 1d; and 129 constables received £1 1s 6d.

There was a weekly allowance of 5s paid to forty-eight constables who
regularly worked in plain clothes, and one inspector, twelve sergeants and
forty-eight constables received a total of £376 2s 8d 'in lieu of uniform'.
Every officer and constable received 3s per month 'boot money'. The total
monies paid out in salaries and allowances came to £52,345 0s 4d.

The remaining £12,655 included the following expenditures: Clothing, helmets, stocks and armlets cost the force £2,951 0s 2d; lanterns and oil cost £310;
necessities for the infirmary, £400; rates, rents and taxes, £2,993; coals and gas,
£895; repairs to police stations, £300; furniture and bedding, £50; printing and
stationery, £300; and miscellaneous payments, £1,012. The top hats worn by
the first policemen were replaced by helmets in this year of 1866.

The estimated income for the ensuing year was £67,161 9s 2d, which was
derived from the following diverse sources: produce of 8d in the pound on the
assessable rental of the town, amounting to £1,518,332; estimated fines and
penalties, £550; payment out of Bridge House Estate for watching London
and Blackfriars Bridges, £668 4s; payment for men on private service at the
bank, post office, railway, City of London Union, Inland Revenue office,
Times office, Guildhall Justice Rooms, Messrs Gooch & Cousens, Messrs
Parson & Co., and Messrs Kearns, Major & Field, and for assistant gaolers and
omnibus timekeepers, £2,114 4s 8d.[17]

Whilst Manchester's councillors and ratepayers were expressing satisfaction
with the police force's finances, its citizens were becoming increasingly dissat-
isfied with the level of protection afforded them. Letters of complaint began
to appear in the columns of local newspapers. On 18 October 1865, the following letter appeared in the *Manchester Courier*:

May I request you through the medium of your valuable paper to give pub-
licity to the disgraceful scenes which are daily occurring in Deansgate, and

which require immediate legal prevention. Yesterday week, as I was returning from St. John's Church after divine service with my wife and daughter,
I saw two women half-naked and in a state of beastly drunkenness, fighting
with a man in Deansgate. I walked some distance past, with my wife and
daughter, requested them to walk home, and then returned. On my return,
the crowd dispersed for it is but justice to say that the utmost respect is generally paid to a clergyman. I waited, however, until a policeman, constable
no. 105, came up and told me it was impossible for him to prevent such
scenes. On the Monday, I called to see Captain Palin, who, after an hour's
waiting, told me he would do his best to ensure order.

Yesterday, however, as I was returning in a cab to St. Johns to perform a
funeral service, I saw two men with their coats off fighting in Deansgate.
Having no time to wait, I requested the driver to go on, which he did with
some difficulty, through a crowd of fifty to one hundred persons, who were
looking-on shouting, many of them encouraging the combatants. Today,
I called again on Captain Palin who said to me that it was impossible for
him, with the force at his disposal, to maintain law and order. It became,
therefore, a question [of] whether mob rule or the law of the land is to
prevail in Manchester.
Signed. W.M. Huntington. Rev'd at St. Johns Church.

Four days later, another letter appeared in the same newspaper. It read:

Sir, the public generally are much indebted to Mr Huntington for calling
their attention to the state and discipline of the police force, more especially at the present period, with winter approaching, when the efficiency of
such a force is of vital importance to us all. Mr. Huntington's letter has also
been the means of eliciting the important fact, which I would otherwise
have doubted, that there is actually a superintendent of police in or near
Manchester. From the ill-disciplined and irregular way in which the police
walk, or rather stray about the streets, I should have supposed that they had
no commander, but were merely left to follow their own will and pleasure. Instead of policemen pacing the streets separately as in other towns,
you seldom meet a policeman who is not accompanied by another, and at
many of the corners of the streets you may observe three of them gossip-
ing together. No doubt it is more agreeable to most policemen, like other
people, to walk in pairs than to wander alone, but we do not pay police to
do what is most pleasant to themselves but to protect our persons and our
property from such outrages as those of which Mr. Huntington complains.

It is obvious that if the police are properly dispersed about, half the present force would be as efficient as the entire force now is.

Signed, A ratepayer.

The Chief Constable was moved to reply to Rev. Huntington's letter in the *Courier*:

Unfortunately, the police have abundant occupation in that district of Deansgate and to prove that they are not inattentive to their duties, it is only necessary to say that on reference to the books I find between the 1st September and the 18th October last, no fewer than 411 persons were taken into custody in and around Deansgate.

However, the Chief Constable's reassurances did little to stem the flow of criticism. On 14 July 1866, another letter of complaint was published in the *Courier*, this time referring to an incident on the banks of the Ashton Canal in Canal Street, Ancoats, where a boy was discovered by two patrolling policemen bathing in the muddy waters:

The officers proceeded to stone the boy in an attempt to get him to climb out of the water. An immense crowd gathered and great indignation was expressed at the conduct of the policemen. It was discovered that the boy was severely cut and bruised and two of the wounds were said to be large enough to lay a finger in. Meanwhile, the street had become alive with people and was literally 'in arms'. The lad was taken to a shed where he had a fit. The police were mobbed and hooted at in the most vigorous fashion, and were in turn treated to a case of stoning, which speedily made them take flight. The lad was wrapped-up in a shirt and taken to the Royal Infirmary.

The Chief Constable's report to the Watch Committee, in 1870, shows that he had already begun a calculated 'clear-out' of 'inefficient and unsuitable officers' with the object of building a more efficient and effective force. He stressed that the pay was good in comparison with other forces in the Northern district, and only three forces paid a higher rate to constables. The establishment now had a staff of 737, with the average length of service standing at six years and nine months. Recruitment had more than compensated for the depletions brought about by dismissals and resignations, and the Chief Constable highlighted that ten years earlier (1860) he had been forced to dismiss forty-one officers, whereas in 1870 only seven officers were dismissed.

During the previous two years, 233 men had joined the force; 300 men had been in the force under ten years; ninety-nine from ten to fifteen years; fifty-eight from fifteen to twenty years; and forty-seven had completed twenty years or more.

The overall strength of the force had more than kept pace with the rising population during the period 1843–70. In 1843, for example, the size of the force was 398 and the population was 239,139, a ratio of 590 persons per policeman. In 1870, the 737 men in the force were attendant upon 374,993 inhabitants, a ratio of 508 persons per policeman, which was well within the recommended level set by the Inspectorate.

During the ten-year period 1860–70, the policeman's workload appears to have increased quite significantly. In 1860, the number of people proceeded against for both summary and indictable offences stood at 10,194. By 1870, this figure had more than doubled to 26,084. Importantly, Peel's preventive principle of policing was very much to the fore in Palin's priorities. In 1869, for example, 1,369 persons were apprehended for 6,794 indictable crimes, compared to the 1870 figures of 1,365 apprehensions for 5,744 indictable crimes.

What is remarkable about this reported reduction in indictable crimes is that this was at a time when Manchester's labouring poor were still crowded in the most densely populated central districts of the city, where living conditions were often deplorable. For example, in 1870, Manchester's population of 374,993 was crowded in an area so small that the official density figure of 83.6 was second only to Liverpool in the national table. By comparison, Salford's density figure was 23.5, Bolton's figure was 47.2, and London's 41.2.

In the year 1870, the Manchester City police force was divided into five territorial divisions. The A Division had its headquarters at Knott Mill, on Deansgate, with 212 men under the command of Superintendent John Gee. The B Division had its headquarters at Goulden Street, Collyhurst, with 159 men under the command of Superintendent Charles William Godby. The C Division had its headquarters at Fairfield Street, with 153 men under the command of Superintendent Thomas Anderton. The D Division had its headquarters at Cavendish Street, with 164 men under the command of Superintendent Thomas Meade. And the E Division was made up of the newly constituted detective branch, with fifty officers under the command of Superintendent Robert Coy.

The force's headquarters were housed in the old town hall building in King Street until 1877, which was the year when the new town hall was opened in Albert Square. The Chief Constable and his administrative staff took up accommodation on the ground floor of the building, with the basement housing a charge office and cells, with direct admittance being gained from Lloyd Street.

In the same year that the new town hall building was opened, a new and substantial divisional headquarters building was under construction in Willert Street, Collyhurst. The case for a new police station in Collyhurst had been made after a series of attacks on policemen and police stations in the district, the most recent being at Goulden Street and nearby Kirby Street. The station design was likened more to a fortress than any conventional police station. Walls were constructed to an extra thickness, and reinforcing metal plates were inserted into the brickwork. Windows were excluded from all ground-floor walls facing public thoroughfares.

The Chief Constable's report of 1870 refers to plain-clothes' allowances being paid to officers in the 'detectives' office', suggesting that the force had by now established a criminal investigation department. However, most of the time spent out of uniform and in plain clothes was to supervise and inspect the various licence-holders in the city, whether in public houses or in the markets. Detective Chief Inspector Caminada mentions in his memoirs that he had just become a member of the detectives' office in 1868, when a prisoner managed to escape from the Knott Mill police station. Evidently it was around this time that the notion of specialist police officers carrying out criminal investigations, out of uniform, was attracting attention.

It is understood that the first Criminal Investigations Department to be staffed exclusively with a trained, full-time staff, backed up by a criminal records office, was set up at Scotland Yard in 1878. This department was established following the 'turf fraud scandal', which had seen three senior police officers charged and convicted of taking bribes from bookmakers. The officers concerned were Chief Inspector Druscovitch, Chief Inspector Palmer and Inspector Meikejohn. The investigations were protracted and complex, and it soon became evident to the Commissioner and the Home Secretary that a fully staffed and trained CID was the way forward.

The very idea of the police operating out of uniform attracted criticism and suspicion from sections of the public, particularly among the working class, who considered it was reminiscent of the old system of government spies and agent provocateurs. Their fears were fuelled by reading stories in popular crime magazines of the exploits of France's first detective, whose name was Vidocq. He had a reputation for corruption and brutality, and would often instigate many of the crimes he claimed to have detected, placing before the courts criminals against whom he had a personal grudge.[18]

Scientific support of police investigations did not gain credibility until the turn of the century. The introduction of fingerprint evidence to identify criminals from the scenes of crime became available to the police in 1901, when the courts finally accepted their reliability. In that year, a burglar in London was convicted by the courts on his identification from a fingerprint found at the scene of the crime. The original concept of fingerprint evidence had been put forward to the Home Office by Sir William Herschel, a Commissioner of Police in Bengal, India, after he had successfully built up a collection of fingerprints which had been used to identify local fraudsters and criminals. Herscel's idea of a system of records being maintained at a 'central police location accessible to dedicated police officers' failed to attract much serious attention until Sir Francis Galton (a cousin of Charles Darwin) made it his business to persuade the Home Secretary of the unique benefits of fingerprints and their importance in criminal identification. Galton was supported by Sir Edward Henry, who devised a new system of clarification, which is still in use today.

In 1901, a fingerprint bureau was established at Scotland Yard, making use of Henry's system. The first provincial fingerprint bureau was opened a few years later at Bradford but it was not until the inter-war years that a national system of record-keeping was established.[19]

The introduction of scientific support for officers in the CID raised the prospects of detection and conviction, which had proved so frustrating for early Chief Constables, who had bemoaned the relatively high numbers of offenders being discharged by the courts. However, applying the scientific advances of the age did not always result in success. Take for example Inspector James Bent, who decided he would 'take advantage of the very latest scientific advances' after attending the scene of a murder at the home of Mr and Mrs Greenwood, in Westbourne Grove, Harpurhey. A maid named Sarah Jane Roberts had been brutally killed and at the scene was found a handwritten letter addressed to Mr Greenwood with a request that he meet the writer at a local public house on the evening of the murder to discuss the sale of some land. As it turned out, the letter writer – who was not known to the Greenwoods – did not show up at the venue and Mr Greenwood returned home to discover the murder. Inspector Bent arranged for the letter to be lithographed, and then published the facsimile in the local and national press with an appeal for readers to identify the writer. It was hoped that identification of the writer would lead the police to the killer, but the appeal was unsuccessful.

During the course of his investigations, the inspector had received a letter from a well-wisher claiming that the very latest scientific advances had shown that the retina in a person's eye kept an image of the last thing that person saw at the time of death. Inspector Bent became convinced that the face of Sarah's killer would be found on her retina.

Excited by this prospect, the inspector made arrangements for a professional photographer – Mr Mudd of St Ann's Square – to attend the undertakers on the day of the funeral, and, before the coffin lid was screwed down, take photographs of the eyes of the murder victim which held an image of her killer. Not surprisingly, the photographs failed to provide any evidence for the hapless Inspector Bent, who was faced with a hefty bill for the services of a top-class photographer. The investigation continued and several local men were arrested but no one was ever charged with the murder of Sarah Jane Roberts.[20]

At the end of the year 1878, Chief Constable Palin tendered his resignation to the Watch Committee after completing twenty-one years in the police. His last years in office had been plagued with ill-health and many of his duties had been carried out by his deputy, Charles Malcolm Wood. A successor had to be found and the Watch Committee lost no time in finding the right man for the job.

Notes

1. *Manchester Guardian*, 24 February 1838.
2. T.A. Critchley, *A History of Police in England and Wales*, 1978, p.47.
3. D. Hurd, *Robert Peel*, 2001, pp.104–5.
4. Constabulary Police Commissioners' report, 1839, p.180.
5. D. Hurd, *Robert Peel*, 2001.
6. *Manchester Guardian*, 18 July 1839.
7. S. Simon, *A Century of City Government*, 1938, p.330.
8. W.R. Cockcroft, 'Liverpool Police 1836–62', article in P. Bell (ed.), *Victorian Lancashire*, 1974, p.154.
9. Manchester Parish Table Book, 4 May 1840.
10. Ibid.
11. S. Simon, *A Century of City Government*, 1938, p.331.
12. A.B. Reach, *Manchester and the Textile Districts in 1849*, 1849, p.160.
13. A. Kidd, *Manchester*, 1993, p.71.
14. P. Wentworth, *History and Annals of Blackley and Neighborhood*, 1892.
15. *Illustrated London News*, 24 May 1843.
16. D. Taylor, *999 and All That*, 1968, p.53.
17. *Manchester Gazette and Times*, 19 December 1867.
18. J. Morton, *The First Detective*, 2005.
19. T.A. Critchley, *A History of Police in England and Wales*, 1978, p.162.
20. J. Bent, *Reminiscences of 42 Years as a Police Officer*, 1880.

8

IRISH FENIANS AND THE MURDER OF A MANCHESTER POLICEMAN

The Fenian movement, otherwise known as the Irish Republican Brotherhood, was a secret society built on what remained of the Young Ireland Movement, which had been defeated by the authorities in Ireland in 1848. Its ranks included many officers of Irish descent who had fought in the American Civil War. Their primary object was the overthrow of the British government in Ireland by armed insurrection.

Fenian activity came to the shores of England in 1867. Their first operation was an aborted bomb attack on Chester Castle. This was followed by an attempted rescue of four Fenian prisoners held at Clerkenwell prison in London, which involved exploding a bomb against the wall of the prison. On this occasion, no damage was caused and no one was injured. A wave of bombings took place against London targets, including an attempt at Scotland Yard. A result of this wave of bombings was the establishment of the Metropolitan Police Special Branch. At first, it was named the Special Irish Branch, but later became known as the Special Branch.[1]

A Fenian outrage with tragic consequences occurred in Manchester on 18 September 1867, when around thirty Irishmen attacked a horse-drawn prison van in Hyde Road, Belle Vue, as it transported seven prisoners, two of whom were leading members of the Fenian movement, from the courts in Manchester to the prison in Belle Vue. During the attack, one of the police officers on duty was shot and killed and another shot and wounded. Three of the attackers were convicted of murder and hanged at the New Bayley prison. Thereafter, the three hanged Fenians came to be known as the Manchester Martyrs.

The number of Fenian supporters in Ireland and in England had fallen significantly by the year 1860 and, as a consequence, Captain Edward O'Meagher Condon had been sent to Manchester in the spring of 1867 to try to rejuvenate the nine sections scattered about the city. A number of small sections of supporters were also to be found in Ashton-under-Lyne, Oldham and Lees.

According to Doughty,[2] Condon set about a reorganisation of the Fenian movements in the Manchester area 'with some gusto'. In order to boost the morale of its supporters, he organised a meeting to be addressed by the movement's senior leadership in Ireland, Colonel Thomas J. Kelly and Captain Timothy Deasy. The meeting was successful and Kelly and Deasy stayed behind in Manchester to be entertained by Condon.

On 18 September 1867, Kelly, Deasy, Condon and some of their supporters were seen by a patrolling constable acting suspiciously as they made their way past the stalls in Shudehill Market in the direction of a house in nearby Oak Street, next to the Band in the Wall public house. The suspects were next seen entering the house in Oak Street, which was occupied by Henry Wilson, a dealer in second-hand clothing. By now, the constable had become even more suspicious, as he knew that Wilson associated with local criminals. He alerted Sergeant Brears, who arranged for those constables on duty in the area to be deployed close by and await further instructions. Around midnight, Kelly and Deasy stepped out of the front door of the house and into Shudehill, where they were immediately confronted by the waiting police officers. Each prisoner was found to be in possession of a loaded revolver. They claimed their names were Wright and Wilson and that they were American citizens.

Both men were arrested and appeared before the Magistrates' Court the following morning, charged with loitering with intent to commit a felony, and possession of illegal firearms. The magistrates ordered that they be remanded in custody for seven days, without anyone in the court realising their true identities.

Meanwhile, their associates and supporters made preparations to rescue them from the custody of the police and set about identifying a suitable location along the route from the courts to the prison at Belle Vue. As it was suspected that the police escort might be armed, Condon sent William Darragh to Birmingham to buy revolvers from a Fenian sympathiser.

It is estimated that between thirty and forty Irishmen were recruited to carry out the rescue operation, and ten of them were armed with revolvers. The most suitable location selected for carrying out the attack on the escorting party was just below the railway bridge across Hyde Road at Belle Vue.

On their reappearance at the Magistrates' Court, the magistrates were told by Superintendent Maybury that enquiries with Scotland Yard had revealed the true identities of the two prisoners and that a warrant of arrest had been issued in Ireland which was now in his possession. He requested that the prisoners be further remanded in custody so that arrangements could be made for their transfer to Ireland. The magistrates agreed to the police application and the two prisoners, now identified as being Kelly and Deasy, were taken down the steps from the dock to the cells below. They were placed in the charge of Sergeant Charles Brett, a policeman with twenty years' service in the Manchester police force, who was to take command of the escorting party as it made its way to the prison. Sergeant 'E1' Brett was the regular escorting officer for prisoners on remand and was popularly known as 'Charlie'.

What followed on that fateful Wednesday afternoon can be drawn from witness statements, which were later presented in evidence to the courts.[3] At 3.30 p.m., the prison van was loaded with seven prisoners, including the two Irishmen and two 12-year-old juveniles, who were named as Joseph Partington, charged with stealing 1s from his employer and James Baxter, charged with vagrancy. These two boys were to be dropped off at the Ardwick Industrial School en route to the prison. There were also three women: Emma Halliday and Ellen Cooper, both charged with larceny, and Frances Armstrong, charged with drunkenness.

Constable Matt Knox was the nominated driver of the horse-drawn van and Sergeant Brett was seated in the rear with the prisoners. Following behind was an escort party of eight constables, none of whom were armed.

Hannah Pennington, wife of the landlord of the Halfway House, Hyde Road, testified that at lunchtime several 'rough looking men' entered the bar of the public house and ordered drinks. She described them as being 'of the lowest class of Irish'. They remained in the public house until mid-afternoon, when they were joined by another group of Irishmen. She particularly noticed 'a tall man, pale faced with a salt and pepper coat and brown pot hat'. This man turned out to be William Philip Allen, who was to play a prominent role in the attack on the prison van.

These men left the Halfway House around three o'clock and walked up a grassy bank next to the railway arches on Hyde Road, where they were observed by locals 'behaving suspiciously'. One of the spotters was William Hully, landlord of the Railway Inn, who testified to seeing 'around thirty roughly dressed men' congregating under the arches.

As the horse-drawn prison van passed under the railway arches, two of the rescuers ran out, grabbed hold of the reins and shot both horses dead. Chaos then followed, with members of the public and rescuers exchanging abuse and throwing stones at one another. Some locals joined with the constables on the escort party and rushed forward, only to retreat fairly rapidly when shots were fired in their direction. Constable Seth Bromley was shot in his leg and a local man named Prosson was wounded.

Despite the commotion outside, Sergeant Brett refused demands to hand over the keys, which were being made through the grille on the rear door. The women were screaming loudly as the muzzle of a pistol was thrust through the grille and a shot was fired. Sergeant Brett sustained a serious head wound and collapsed. One of the women grabbed the bunch of keys and handed them through the grille. The van door was then unlocked and the two Fenian prisoners, Kelly and Deasy, climbed over Sergeant Brett and escaped, leaving the other terrified prisoners screaming and confused at the scene.

Constable Knox went to the assistance of Sergeant Brett and he was taken from the scene to the Infirmary, where he died from his head wound at 5.30 the next morning.

Members of the crowd of onlookers joined with policemen from the escort and chased after the fleeing rescuers and the freed prisoners. One of the first to be captured was Michael Larkin, who had been lagging behind the main group. Next to be detained was Captain Michael O'Brien, followed by William Allen. A total of forty-one men were eventually arrested and taken into custody. At the end of the day, Kelly and Deasy were still at large. Witnesses to the events included: George Pickup, a brick-maker, who assisted in the capture of several Irishmen; Thomas Paterson, a puddler, who identified Allen as being armed with two pistols; John Griffiths, a hairdresser, whose shop was in Hyde Road, who identified Allen, gave chase and assisted in his capture; and George Mulholland, aged 12, who came forward and testified that he had overheard conversations between Allen and Larkin and had heard Allen shout at the driver, 'Stop or I'll blow your brains out.'

Five men were charged with murdering Sergeant Brett. They were: William Allen, William Gould (Michael O'Brien), Michael Larkin, Edward Shore (Condon), and Thomas Maguire. Mr Justice Blackburn and Mr Justice Mellor were appointed to hear the case at the Assize Courts, with the Attorney General, Sir John Kerslake, appearing for the prosecution. At the end of the proceedings, all were convicted and sentenced to be hanged at Strangeways prison. Maguire was subsequently pardoned by the Home Secretary and Condon's sentence was commuted to life imprisonment.

On 23 November 1867, the sentence of the Assize Court was carried out and Allen, Gould and Larkin were hanged at Strangeways.

It is believed that both of the prisoners who escaped from the police escort evaded capture by being transported from Manchester to America in the days that followed. Both were to live out the rest of their lives in New York. Deasy was reported to have died in 1880 and Kelly in 1908.

According to the memoirs of Lafargue, the son-in-law of Karl Marx, Sinn Feiners were sheltered by Mary Burns (partner of Frederick Engels) at their house just off Deansgate, until a safe passage could be arranged. Lafargue wrote: 'More than one Sinn Feiner found hospitality in Engels' house and it was thanks to his wife that their leader, in the attempt to free condemned Sinn Feiners on the way to the scaffold, was also to evade the police.'[4]

The funeral of Sergeant Brett took place on 29 September at Harpurhey Cemetery. It attracted a large crowd, estimated at 15,000, which included many Irish people who had been genuinely outraged by the circumstances of his death. The Mayor of Manchester attended and headed the procession of mourners, alongside the Chief Constable, Captain Palin, as the cortège made its way from the Brett household in Wilson Street to the cemetery.

Concerns were raised that something had gone tragically wrong with police security on 18 September. The reputation of the force did not rate as highly as the acts of bravery by its individual officers. 'I have never been so annoyed,' wrote the Home Secretary Mr Hardy, after receiving news of the rescue. He blamed the force's command for failing to respond positively to a telegram sent on the day of the rescue by the Chief Secretary to the Dublin government (Lord Mayo), addressed to Superintendent Maybury of the Manchester police. It was sent at 1.30 p.m., received in the Manchester Post Office at 1.55 p.m. and delivered to police headquarters at 2.05 p.m. The telegram read: 'Are the prisoners lodged in gaol? Have every precaution taken for their safe custody. Let extra guards be provided. If necessary, consult with Williamson [a Fenian expert living in England].'

Superintendent Maybury was not on duty at this time and a junior clerk opened and read the telegram. It was then handed over to the inspector on duty at 2.15 p.m. The inspector went in search of the senior operational officer on duty, which was another superintendent, to whom he handed over the telegram. The superintendent directed that eight constables provide an escorting party for the prison van, and another four constables were to follow close behind. Sergeant Brett was nominated to be in charge of the prisoners inside the van. The police officers on duty were not issued with firearms.[5]

The Dublin telegram does not specifically mention firearms being used, or that there was intelligence that an attack was being planned. However, the fact that it was now known that the prisoners were leaders of an armed insurrectionary movement perhaps should have induced the police to seriously consider arming some, if not all, escorting officers. Indeed, that was the view of the Home Secretary, who laid the blame for this tragic episode at the door of the Manchester police force.

In the year 1877, a giant stone memorial was erected in St Joseph's Cemetery, Moston, to commemorate the 'Manchester Martyrs', and every year thereafter, the deaths of Allen, Gould and Larkin are commemorated by a march through the streets of Manchester to the cemetery, attended by a small band of supporters.

The response of members of the local community in assisting the police at the scene, and their involvement in the capture of some of the armed perpetrators, suggests that by this time any hostility towards the local police had by now subsided, if not completely evaporated. It appears that the officers on duty were identified as being *their* police rather than being perceived as agents of the government.

Notes

1. C. Emsley, *The Great British Bobby*, 2009, p.164.
2. J. Doughty, *The Manchester Outrage: A Fenian Tragedy*, 2001.
3. L. O'Broin, *Fenian Fever*, 1971.
4. Professor C. Bloom, *The Taste for Terror*, 2010, p.177.
5. L. O'Broin, *Fenian Fever*, 1971.

9

SCANDAL AND CORRUPTION: A STRUGGLE FOR CONTROL AND INDEPENDENCE

Manchester's Watch Committee, made up of councillors and aldermen, secured a measure of control over the Chief Constable and his police force by retaining the power to appoint, promote and discipline all its police officers. Sadly, this power was to prove corrupting and was abused to such an extent that a public scandal broke out that engulfed members of the committee and its Chief Constable.

Membership of the local council at the time proved attractive to local businessmen for a variety of reasons. Apart from power, prestige and a sense of *noblesse oblige*, there were many shopkeepers, tradesman and 'brewery interests', who were motivated by a desire to benefit from a privileged access to information that might protect their own interests. Towards the end of the century, the writer Beatrice Webb visited Manchester and was less than impressed with the quality and standards of Manchester's councillors. She wrote: 'The social status is predominantly lower middle-class. The abler administrators have no pretension to ideas, hardly any grammar, and are merely hard-headed shopkeepers divided in their minds between a desire to keep the rates down and their ambition to magnify the importance of Manchester.'[1]

In 1879, members of the Watch Committee decided to appoint Charles Malcolm Wood as the city's next Chief Constable. Mr Wood was just 34 years of age and had spent the previous six months as Mr Palin's deputy. The son of a senior civil servant, Mr Wood had joined the Indian civil service after leaving school. During his time in India, he was appointed Assistant Superintendent of the Sindh police in Karachi.

The new Chief Constable's term of office came to be dominated by the misconduct of one of his senior officers. The controversy began in 1882, when a vacancy arose for a superintendent in the South Manchester district. The Chief Constable compiled a shortlist of suitable candidates to be interviewed by the Watch Committee. However, when the list was returned to him, so he could make the necessary arrangements for candidates to attend for interview, an additional name had been included. The name of Inspector William Bannister, a junior officer working at the Cavendish Street police station, had been added to the list without consultation. The Chief Constable protested to Alderman Bennett, the chairman of the committee, that this officer was unqualified for such a promotion, but he was overruled and Bannister was called for interview. To the amazement of the Chief Constable and his fellow senior officers, Bannister was selected by the Watch Committee for promotion to the rank of superintendent.[2]

During the next ten years, 'the audacity of this bold, bad man went largely unchecked', as the morale and reputation of the force's D Division became the talk of the force and many parts of the city. It all came to a head in 1892, when Bannister's association with the owner of a disorderly house was made the subject of a critical report in the local press.[3] A public outcry resulted in the council calling for a public inquiry into the affair, but Alderman Bennett successfully blocked the move, insisting that the Watch Committee was well placed to deal with the matter internally without recourse to a public inquiry. The council relented and authorised Alderman Bennett and his committee to investigate and report its findings.

The Watch Committee began to hear evidence against Superintendent Bannister on charges of misconduct. Bannister took the unusual step of calling his young daughter to support his claim that he was visiting the house in Shepley Street in connection with a will, in which both he and the lady concerned were beneficiaries. At the conclusion of the hearing, the committee, by a slim majority, found him not guilty and, despite protestations made by the Chief Constable and dissenting members of the Watch Committee who had sought his dismissal, Alderman Bennett insisted that Superintendent Bannister be reinstated to his post on the D Division.

It would seem, however, that Bannister failed to learn any lessons from this experience and, by 1897, his conduct once again became the source of public scandal. On this occasion, repeated complaints of drunkenness, and visits to disorderly houses to collect 'rents' against the threat of prosecution, were to prove so embarrassing that the council demanded a full public inquiry be carried out into the affairs of the D Division. Once again Alderman Bennett tried to oppose such a move but this time he was overruled. The formal procedure began with the Lord Mayor requesting that the Home Secretary set up a public inquiry and appoint a suitable person to act as chairman.

Mr J.S. Dugdale, QC was appointed to conduct the review, which was held in the Manchester Magistrates' Court building, where evidence from witnesses was taken on oath. The Inquiry heard many adverse comments from police officers regarding Bannister's appointment to the rank of superintendent, and his continuation in that rank after his first brush with the Watch Committee in 1892. It became abundantly clear that the relationship between the Watch Committee and the Chief Constable had become extremely strained after the committee ignored the Chief Constable's recommendation and promoted a police constable to the rank of sergeant, on the personal recommendation of Superintendent Bannister, despite evidence being presented that showed that the constable had been fined five times for drunken behaviour whilst on duty.

A number of police witnesses testified that they felt too many of Manchester's councillors, including Alderman Bennett, were unsuitable to be members of the Watch Committee because of their interests in the liquor licensing trade.[4]

Police witnesses also made accusations that Bannister shielded owners of disorderly houses from prosecution, which were additional to those which featured in the charges. Drunkenness was endemic among officers on the D Division, especially those in the senior ranks, who were also prone to demanding money from junior ranks. One police witness provided evidence which showed that the division's statistical returns 'were a farce', particularly those figures relating to public houses and prostitution.[5]

In his evidence to the Inquiry, the Chief Constable stated that he took great exception to the interferences made by members of the committee: 'When it came to promotions, I think that I ought to have [had] all the appointments. I cannot be held responsible for men appointed by the watch committee or anyone else.' When asked whether he refused to take any responsibility for Bannister's conduct, the Chief Constable answered: 'I will not take the responsibility of any man whom I say is put in a position which he ought not to have.'

Once he had heard all of the evidence, the Inquiry chairman submitted to the Home Secretary his interim report with recommendations for future action. The initial response of the Home Secretary was to write to the Chief Constable advising him that in future he should consider directly controlling all police appointments and promotions, and remove this functional responsibility from the hands of the Watch Committee. The Chief Constable's reply surprised even his most ardent supporters, in that he went against all that he had said to the Committee of Inquiry. Mr Wood wrote: 'This method of appointment and promotion was already virtually the practice in Manchester and has been for sometime.'

The Inquiry's final report found Superintendent Bannister guilty of the charges of gross misconduct, and made recommendations that disciplinary charges be made against several other police officers. The report concluded: 'It is perhaps not premature to congratulate the city upon the great fact, at any rate, that the large majority of the police have no complaint against them whatsoever and that the offences and malpractices were confined to just one division.'

Members of the Watch Committee were sufficiently shaken by the Inquiry's findings of 'gross misconduct' to consider resigning as a body; the motion was lost by just two votes. Subsequently, however, the committee's chairman, Alderman Bennett, did resign and the city council determined that all members of the Watch Committee must face reselection by ballot.

Fourteen constables from the D Division resigned voluntarily; twelve others were called upon to resign, and thirteen were dismissed, including Superintendent Bannister. A total of forty police officers left the force as a result of the Dugdale Inquiry. Attempts were made by those officers 'required to resign' to lodge appeals with the Watch Committee, but such a course of action was rejected by the full council.

The findings and recommendations of the Dugdale Inquiry resurfaced when the newly elected Watch Committee decided to reconsider all of the Dugdale Inquiry findings and went on to review all resignations and dismissals. At its conclusion, the committee announced that it was to 'extend leniency' to those officers who had been disciplined as a result of the Inquiry, but this act of clemency did not extend to Bannister. And, in another challenge to the Inquiry and to the Home Secretary, the Watch Committee announced that it would retain in its own hands the appointment, promotion and discipline of all officers in the force, 'after having due consultation with the Chief Constable'.

Not surprisingly, on hearing the news of this apparent about-turn, the Home Secretary was extremely annoyed, but was constitutionally powerless to overrule the council's decision. However, politically he possessed a most powerful weapon in the form of the financial police grant, which was paid annually to the force and amounted to 80 per cent of expenditure. The Home Secretary responded by announcing that he was withholding next year's grant until he was fully satisfied that the efficiency of the Manchester force was of a high standard. In practice, this meant the force undergoing a full inspection conducted by the Inspectorate, whose decision on whether or not to certify that they had reached the required standard of efficiency would be presented to the Home Secretary for his consideration.

It appears that the Chief Constable's health suffered as a consequence of these long drawn-out inquiries. A report was submitted to the Watch Committee which stated that the Chief Constable was in poor health and requesting that he be granted a period of sick leave. The committee granted his request and instructed that he take a period of six months paid leave from the force to help in his recovery. At the end of the six months, the Chief Constable tendered his resignation, which the Watch Committee accepted with regret and, as a token of their appreciation, granted him a full pension of £500.

Mr Wood's departure closed this embarrassing chapter in the force's history. Yet to be resolved, however, was the thorny relationship between the Chief Constable and the Watch Committee, the constitutional origins of which are an historical legacy of common law. In essence, the common law position is that constables are accountable only to the law, and no body or individual can instruct a constable that he must or must not prosecute this man or that one, nor is he the servant of anyone save the law itself.[6] Under the terms of the Municipal Corporations Act, the Watch Committee of a local borough council was empowered to establish a police force and to make regulations 'for preventing neglect or abuse and for rendering constables efficient in the discharge of their duties', with the added provision for the dismissal of those constables 'whom they shall think negligent in the discharge of their duties'. The extent to which a Watch Committee interfered in the executive control of the force depended largely on their relationship with their Chief Constable. In the nineteenth century, the subordination of a Chief Constable to the Watch Committee was part of common understanding in some borough forces, but not so in county forces, where Chief Constables were found not to be subjected to the same political controls.[7]

Meanwhile, the Home Secretary restored the police grant the following year. This decision had more to do with the choice of a new Chief Constable than with the level of 'efficiency' in the Manchester force. It was the firm belief of the Home Office that the new appointment's reputation and stature was set to rebalance the tripartite system of police control and accountability.

Notes

1. S. Simon, *A Century of City Government*, 1938, p.399.
2. Dugdale Inquiry Minutes, p.96.
3. Ibid., p.44.
4. Ibid., p.98.
5. Ibid., p.1.
6. Restated in Lord Denning's *obiter* in the first of the Blackburn trials.
7. T.A. Critchley, *A History of Police in England and Wales*, 1978.

10

AN INDEPENDENT CHIEF CONSTABLE

Robert Peacock had been a career policeman who joined the Bradford Borough police force as a 19-year-old constable. Nine years later he was appointed as Chief Constable of the Canterbury police force. In 1892, he transferred to the Oldham Borough force and spent six years in that post before successfully applying for the Manchester vacancy in March 1898. The move was an attractive one financially, with his salary increasing from £400 to £800.

All too aware of the difficulties faced by his predecessor, Peacock set about introducing changes to the system of promotions, insisting that in future all promotions in Manchester would be made by examination and interview and that he, as the Chief Constable, would chair interviewing panels. The Watch Committee were in agreement and, by a majority, sanctioned the Chief Constable's proposals, which in effect transferred their powers of control over these proceedings.

Peacock recognised that if his policy was to work, he would need to raise the numeracy and literacy standards in the force. His immediate task, therefore, was to introduce educational classes for all members of the force.

At a conference of police officers held on 15 September 1899, the Chief Constable explained his policy:

It gives me the greatest pleasure to be present this afternoon to open the first session of educational classes ever formed in the Manchester City force and it is very gratifying, both to members of the watch committee and to myself, to find that so many members of the force have decided to avail themselves of the opportunity now presented of improving themselves educationally. I am looking forward to the time in the near future when every man will be able to write, compose and properly complete his own reports. I have no desire to criticise the watch committee or chief constables of the past, but I can assure you, most emphatically, promotions will be made solely on merit.

The Chief Constable's policies were not well received by everyone connected with the force, with some members of the local council and the magistrates' bench prepared to challenge him through the courts. In 1901, a dispute arose between the police and some members of the magistrates' bench. The issue involved William Thompson, a publican and magistrate from Beswick, who had been summonsed for permitting drunkenness on his licensed premises. Two of his fellow magistrates made repeated, but unsuccessful, attempts to persuade the police to drop the charges against their colleague. They went on to rearrange their rotas so that they would be sitting on the bench when the charges against their fellow magistrate were heard. This conduct was brought to the notice of the Chief Constable, who successfully applied for the case to be adjourned and then submitted a critical report to members of the Watch Committee who convened a special meeting. Their response was to circulate the Chief Constable's report to the chairman of the magistrates' bench, the Chancellor of the Duchy of Lancaster, and to the Home Secretary. The outcome was that the two magistrates were forced to resign from the bench and the publican, William Thompson, was convicted of all charges.

Two years later, two prominent members of the city's elite became locked in a legal dispute with the Chief Constable, going so far as to openly challenge his honesty and integrity. The parties involved were Mr John Pitt Hardacre, manager of the Comedy Theatre, and his close friend Councillor Ross Clyne. It transpired that Pitt Hardacre had applied to the magistrates for the renewal of his liquor and theatrical licence, which had been refused following complaints made by the Chief Constable that he had repeatedly allowed prostitutes to frequent his premises. Witness evidence was provided by Police Constable Joseph Lyon and a local woman named Gertrude Reynolds.

Pitt Hardacre retaliated by making an application to the court for summonses to be issued against all three parties involved, alleging a criminal conspiracy and the falsification of evidence. The magistrates refused to grant such an application.

Councillor Ross Clyne then joined with his friend in alleging that the Chief Constable was himself a person of ill-repute and had exceeded his statutory authority when objecting to Pitt Hardacre's application for the renewal of his licences. The two men also alleged that Mr Peacock had falsified his age when he applied for the post of Chief Constable, so that his pension would be increased. The charges were of sufficient gravity that, if substantiated, they could result in the Chief Constable's dismissal.

The city council decided they would deal with the matter internally, and refused demands for the matter to be referred to the Home Secretary. After listening to all the evidence presented by the lawyer representing the two men, the council dismissed the charges as being 'without foundation' and exonerated the Chief Constable from any blame. They then called upon Councillor Ross Clyne to resign immediately from his position on the council.[1]

After stepping out from under these clouds of suspicion and legal challenges, the Chief Constable returned to the business of reforming the force with renewed vigour. He reported to the Watch Committee that as the nature and workload of his force had changed dramatically from what it had been twenty years before, he needed additional manpower to meet the new challenges. A major problem, he reported, was the increase in motor traffic on the city's streets, which required extra policemen to man the busiest road junctions. By the end of the year 1899, the number of fixed traffic points had increased from twenty-three to fifty-six. He reported:

> I need an additional thirty officers. The number required cannot be drawn from the men at present available for street duty unless the men are taken from their beats, which, if anything, are much too long at present, and already a number of the beats have had to be doubled, that is, one man having to work two beats.

The Chief Constable identified sixteen non-operational posts that were to be scrapped, with the post-holders being transferred to beat duties: 'So far, twelve constables working in the courts have been transferred to street duties, the number of Coroner's officers has been reduced from three to two and the three constables on security duties in the town hall have been transferred to street duties.'

The remnants of the pre-motorcar age were still making demands on his force, however. For example, the Chief Constable reported that his officers had impounded 373 horses, which had either been found straying, or else their drivers had been arrested for being drunk. There were also 573 hand-carts, coal-wagons and carriages impounded.

Despite an increase in responsibilities linked to traffic congestion, the Chief Constable stated that there had been a gradual reduction in the number of crimes reported in the first years of the twentieth century. For example, in 1913, a total of 2,612 criminal offences had been reported – made up of violence against the person, larceny and criminal damage – which represented a reduction of fifty-one offences when compared with the previous year.

Robert Peacock embraced Peel's concept of 'policing by consent', which he envisaged as being the litmus test of an effective police force, and seized every opportunity to promote what he saw as 'real community policing'. In an article published in the *Manchester Evening News*, he pointed out:

> The force that was once a power drastic enough to leave its mark on the minds of our grandfathers and mothers has changed. No longer is it feared. Today, it is something that has become a friend to the community; the force has engrained itself in the goodwill of its citizens until this boast of friendship, a real friendship between police and public, has become an established fact.[2]

Robert Peacock went on to serve as Chief Constable of Manchester for twenty-eight years, before his sudden death in 1926. The editor of the *Manchester Evening News* described him as 'the doyen of all Chief Constables'. He was knighted in 1923.

In conclusion, the nineteenth century saw a transformation of English society the like of which had never been seen before. Manchester was positioned in the centre of this great age of industrialisation and maintained its dominant position up to the First World War.

Predictions of a revolution never materialised, even though Manchester possessed all of the preconditions, according to Engels. No doubt the 'exploited and alienated' working class found some support through religious worship; a host of self-help schemes, such as the co-operative movement; education through Sunday schools and Mechanics' Institutes; as well as material benefits from the repeal of the Corn Laws. Of course, there is always the possibility that the analysis which determined that a revolution was 'inevitable' was itself flawed from the very beginning, and that rather than developing a 'class consciousness', the ideas and demands of Manchester's working class were essentially economic, seeking little more than improved wages and conditions. This is not to discredit what Engels had to say about Manchester and the emergence of the two great classes in a capitalist society. After all, the essence of Engels and Marx's analysis lay in the discovery that we are all products of our times, and all times are the products of economics.

It has been shown that the measurement of crime was a complex business, involving many variable factors. The nature and scale of criminal behaviours varied in response to the changes taking place, such as the state's definition of what constitutes a 'crime', the introduction of a professional police, and the introduction of crime-prevention methods such as the installation of street lighting. Any direct correlation between criminal behaviours and economic fluctuations remains unclear and problematic. There is little evidence to support the popular view that high unemployment drives honest members of the working class into crime, or women into prostitution.

The second half of the century saw the cruel and repressive criminal and penal codes subjected to reform in favour of a more humanitarian, liberal system. The concept of 'deterrence' no longer depended on a harsh penal code but relied upon the capacity of a professional police to prevent and detect criminal offences.

This was the period that saw the birth of modern, industrialised and urbanised Manchester. Outstanding events, movements and trends have been highlighted, and so too the contribution made by outstanding individuals such as William Cobbett, Joseph Nadin, Richard Cobden and John Bright. Some of the issues and problems that emerged during the Industrial Revolution remain with us today and it is hoped that this book will, in some small way, inform future debates about crime and maintaining good order in modern, urban societies.

As Winston Churchill wrote, 'The further back I look, the further forward I can see.'

Notes

1. City council proceedings, 5 September 1906, pp.341, 372, 381.
2. *Manchester Evening News*, 9 June 1926.

INDEX

If you enjoyed this book, you may also be interested in…

Greater Manchester Murders
ALAN HAYHURST

Contained within the pages of this book are the stories behind some of the most notorious murders in the history of Greater Manchester. They include the case of cat burglar Charlie Peace, who killed 20-year-old PC Nicolas Cock in Seymour Grove, and only confessed after he had been sentenced to death for another murder; the sad tale of William Robert Taylor, whose young daughter was killed in a boilder explosion and who, later, desperate and in debt, murdered his landlord as well as his three remaining children; and the death of Police Sergeant Charles Brett, who stuck bravely to his post despite an armed attack on his prison van by the 'Manchester Martyrs.'

978 0 7509 5091 6

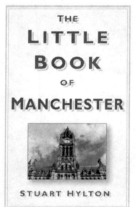

The Little Book of Manchester
STUART HYLTON

An intriguing, fast-paced, fact-packed compendium of places, people and events in the city, from its Roman origins to the present day. Here you can read about the important contributions the city made to the history of the nation, learn about the individual communities and how they came together to form the modern city and meet some of the great men and women, the eccentrics and the scoundrels with which its history is littered. A reliable reference book and quirky guide, its bite-sized chunks of history can be dipped into time and again to reveal some new facts about the story of this amazing city. This is a remarkably engaging little book.

978 0 7524 7947 7

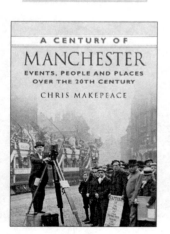

A Century of Manchester
CHRIS MAKEPEACE

This fascinating selection of photographs illustrates the extraordinary transformation that has taken place in Manchester during the twentieth century, offering an insight into the daily lives and living conditions of local people. The book provides a striking account of the changes that have so altered Manchester's appearance and records the process of transformation. Drawing on detailed local knowledge of the community, this book recalls what Manchester has lost in terms of buildings, traditions and ways of life. It also acknowledges the regeneration that has taken place and celebrates the character and energy of local people as they move through the first years of this new century.

978 0 7509 4917 0

Visit our website and discover thousands of other History Press books.

www.thehistorypress.co.uk